Life Is a Dream
La vida es sueño

A Dual-Language Book

Pedro Calderón de la Barca

Edited and Translated by
STANLEY APPELBAUM

DOVER PUBLICATIONS
Garden City, New York

Copyright

Bibliographical Note

This Dover edition, first published in 2002, contains the full Spanish text of *La vida es sueño,* taken from a standard edition. The English translation, Introduction and notes are by Stanley Appelbaum.

The English translation, with a separate set of notes and a different introductory Note (also by Stanley Appelbaum), was published as a Dover Thrift Edition in 2002.

Theatrical Rights

Library of Congress Cataloging-in-Publication Data

Calderón de la Barca, Pedro, 1600–1681.
   [Vida es sueño. English & Spanish]
   Life is a dream = La vida es sueño / Pedro Calderón de la Barca ; translation, publisher's note and notes by Stanley Appelbaum.
      p. cm.
   ISBN-13: 978-0-486-42473-6 (pbk.)
   ISBN-10: 0-486-42473-1 (pbk.)
   I. Title: Vida es sueño. II. Appelbaum, Stanley. III. Title.

PQ6292.V5 A77 2002b
862'.3—dc21

2002073559

Manufactured in the United States of America
42473114   2022
www.doverpublications.com

Contents

Introduction

Spanish Theater in the Time of Calderón

In other areas of Spanish literature the Golden Age (Siglo de Oro) is often taken to include much or all of the sixteenth century, as well as the seventeenth, but in the field of drama it is more or less coextensive with the lifetime of Pedro Calderón de la Barca (1600–1681). Calderón is considered either the greatest or the second greatest dramatist during this highly acclaimed period: some award the palm to the inventiveness and verve of Lope de Vega (1562–1635), others to Calderón's polish and profundity.

Golden Age drama, which in itself was not unchanging and monolithic, did not issue from a vacuum. Play texts in Spanish (that is, Castilian, as opposed to Catalan, etc.) are unusually sparse in the medieval period, in comparison with those in other West European countries, but from about 1500 on, under a strong influence from precocious Italy, important Renaissance playwrights emerged in Spain. The pastoral plays of Juan del Encina (?1468–?1530); the chivalric and religious plays, farces, and masques of Gil Vicente (?1460–?1539, a Portuguese who wrote both in his own language and in Castilian); and the five-act, single-verse-form plays of Bartolomé de Torres Naharro (?1485–?1520) were all written for private performances in royal or noble circles.

By the middle of the sixteenth century, public theaters were active, featuring works by men like Lope de Rueda (?1509–1565), who specialized in one-act prose comedies (*pasos*). As the century progressed, scholarly university plays ("school drama") were put on, and Italian commedia dell'arte troupes toured Spain. The generation before Lope de Vega was dominated by Miguel de Cervantes (1547–1616, author of *Don Quixote*), who wrote both verse tragedies and prose one-acters (*entremeses*), and by Juan de la Cueva

(?1550–1610), whose four-act tragedies are credited with introducing national themes, drawn from ballads and chronicles, into the Spanish theater.

In the era of Lope de Vega, these trends were in full flower, and he himself consolidated and consecrated (though he did not invent them) several features of the *comedia nueva*, or *comedia española*, the chief dramatic form of the period. The following paragraphs summarize the leading characteristics of the *comedia* ("play," not necessarily "comedy") as performed in public in the first four decades of the seventeenth century. (*La vida es sueño* dates from about 1635.)

The playwright (*poeta*) sold his play outright to the actor-manager (*autor*) of an acting company, who most often staged it in a *corral*, a purpose-built theater in an innyard or in a vacant space between existing buildings. Originally the *corrales* were owned and run by religious fraternities, which used the admission money to finance their own hospitals. Later, the *corrales* were leased to companies of actors. (Lope once stated that, in his lifetime, the number of troupes in Madrid had increased from two to forty.) Later still, at least in Madrid, the *corrales* were taken over by the municipality.

A typical *corral* (restored examples exist in Alcalá de Henares and Almagro) was a long rectangle, with the stage at the short side opposite the entrance. The two long sides had galleries for seating, while the groundlings stood in the "pit." The stage had lateral entrances, a simple backcloth, one or two upper levels, and, on the main level, a "discovery space," a small area closed off by doors or curtains that could be opened for significant revelations. (Thus, at the very beginning of *La vida es sueño*, first Rosaura and then Clarín appear on an upper stage level representing the mountainside and descend to the main acting level, where they discover Segismundo in the "discovery space," which represents his cave dungeon at the foot of the mountain.) There was no formal scenery, and just a bare minimum of props, though costuming was important, both for display and for identifying the characters and their (all-important!) station in life.

A new play might be given only two, three, or four performances, so fresh material was in constant demand. Hence, the astronomical number of plays written in the period and, hence, the undue haste that could affect the work of such popular purveyors as Lope. Performances began in the late afternoon and were over by dark. Before and after a *comedia*, and between its acts, the audience was regaled with curtain-raisers, skits, and music.

The subject matter of the *comedia* was quite varied. There were historical plays (from both Spanish and foreign history), plays based on Bible stories and saints' lives, comedies of amorous intrigue abetted by scheming servants, family tragedies, and so on. Certain topics were fashionable at certain times, such as the rash of plays in which lower-class people (like Calderón's Mayor of Zalamea) defend their honor against overbearing authority figures. There were relatively few outright tragedies; in general, even the most serious plays had comic moments, and the final outcome is usually fairly optimistic, with good conquering evil, so that the term "tragicomedy" would apply to those *comedias* that are not strictly comedies in our sense.

Lope's practice assured the victory of the three-act form for the *comedia* in the seventeenth century. The three acts generally contained the exposition, complication, and denouement, respectively. The pseudo-Aristotelian, neoclassical unities of time and place (unchanging locale, 24-hour limit to the action of a play) usually were not observed. As in the Elizabethan public theaters in England, scene changes were fluid and were made known chiefly by means of the dialogue; stage directions in printed texts are sparse and fail to supply locations.

Roles were usually standardized. Acting companies had players who specialized in certain kinds of roles: young hero (*galán*), young heroine (*dama*), old man (*barba*), and so on. Female roles were played by actresses from 1608 on. A role type particularly characteristic of Spanish Golden Age drama is the *gracioso* ("comic"), often a shrewd and witty but selfish, greedy, and cowardly servant or other lower-class figure, a spokesman for the "sensible" but materialistic and circumscribed point of view. The *gracioso* might merely inject punning one-liners, but in the better plays, like *La vida es sueño*, he could be crucial to the action.

One essential aspect of *comedias* that translations disguise, or completely conceal, is that they are in verse, and, in fact (chiefly thanks to Lope), in a variety of verse forms, usually involving rhyme or assonance, that correspond to the content of the dialogue. (See the breakdown of verse forms in *La vida es sueño* later in the Introduction.) In weaker plays, the versification can be facile and routine, but Calderón is unquestionably a first-rate poet.

With some exceptions, scenes of violent action either merely are reported, or are heard as "sound effects" from offstage, and not enacted in the audience's view.

Frequently there are a few "winks" at the audience, such as working the title of the play into the dialogue, or addressing the playgoers directly at the very end, asking their indulgence. (Both features occur in *La vida es sueño*.)

The texts of the *comedias* as originally published do not necessarily represent in every detail what the playwrights wrote. The plays often were printed hastily, and/or pirated, for immediate profit, and the text was sometimes based on the recollections of actors who had played roles in the play. Attributions to authors (who rarely oversaw the publication themselves) often were inaccurate. A successful writer like Lope would be named as author of other men's work in order to deceive the purchaser.

Other major Spanish playwrights, older than Calderón but still active at the beginning of his career, were: Castro (Guillén de Castro y Bellvís, 1569–1631), author of the pair of plays *Las mocedades del Cid* (Youthful Exploits of El Cid), the first of which was the direct basis of Pierre Corneille's *Le Cid*; the Mexican-born Alarcón (Juan Ruiz de Alarcón y Mendoza, ?1580–1639), author of *La verdad sospechosa* (Truth You Can't Trust), the direct basis of Corneille's *Le menteur* (The Liar); and "Tirso de Molina" (Gabriel Téllez, ?1580–1648), who often is credited with the play that is the earliest known work about the Don Juan figure, *El burlador de Sevilla* (The Seducer from Seville).

Important near-contemporaries of Calderón were: Francisco de Rojas Zorrilla (1607–1684), author of *Del rey abajo, ninguno* (No One of Rank Lower Than King); and Agustín Moreto (1618–1669), author of *El desdén con el desdén* (Fighting Scorn with Scorn).

After about 1620 there was a tendency to furnish more scenery in the *corrales*, and the importance of royal and noble private theaters in palaces increased; they colored Calderón's later career extensively. The private theaters featured elaborate, sumptuous staging (often using the know-how of imported Italian engineers) and more scholarly plays, based on Greco-Roman mythology, in which music was an important constituent. (There were musical dramas with spoken dialogue, and also fully sung operas.)

Calderón's literary production would have been much different without the existence of the second-most-important dramatic genre of the era, of which he became the supreme exponent: the *auto sacramental*. The *auto*, which had existed in a more primitive form since at least 1500, was a religious play performed on the feast of Corpus Christi, and thus thematically related to the sacrament of the Eucharist. It was in verse, in one long act, with allegorical characters (like English morality plays), and was staged elaborately in public squares, with decorated floats used as acting areas.

Calderón's Life and Career

Calderón was born in Madrid in 1600 into the lowest rank of the nobility. His father, from Santander in northern Spain, was an accountant in the royal treasury department (even though noblemen weren't supposed to work for a living), and followed the royal court wherever it moved. The father–son conflict in *La vida es sueño* and other Calderón plays is said to stem from the authoritarian nature of the playwright's father. Pedro was slated for a career in the Church because a chaplaincy was hereditary in the family, and he was given the appropriate education.

While Pedro was studying at the Jesuit school in Madrid (1608–1613), his mother died (1610). It is dubious whether he actually wrote his first play when he was thirteen. In 1614, the same year when his father remarried, Pedro entered the University of Alcalá de Henares, but transferred to Salamanca in 1615, the year in which his father died. Orphaned, he became even more closely bonded to his brothers, José and Diego. In 1620, after receiving his degree in canon law (his legal and theological training is manifested in such passages of his works as the scene of hair-splitting casuistry between Rosaura and Clotaldo in the last act of *La vida es sueño*), he made a mark as a poet back in Madrid with a contest poem in honor of the city's new patron saint, Isidore "the Farmer."

Calderón wasn't a retiring man of letters, however, in his younger days. In 1621 he and his beloved brothers were accused of a murder; and, some years later, as a constable, he violated the sanctuary of a convent to seize a malefactor. In 1623 he served in the army in Flanders and Lombardy, but in that same year he enjoyed his first success as a playwright, and made writing for the stage his career, working both for the public *corrales* and for the king's private theaters. His popularity and success were sustained, and in 1636 the king made him a Knight of Santiago. (A papal dispensation was needed for his admittance into that exclusive order, because of his father's low rank and work-sullied hands.)

The playwright temporarily became a soldier again during the 1640–1642 Catalonian Revolt against royal authority, but thereafter his life was more placid, though marked by personal losses that deepened his religious feelings. His brother José died in 1645; Diego, in 1647; and Pedro's mistress, in 1648 (their son died in childhood a few years later). In 1650 Calderón entered the Third Order of Franciscans; he was ordained a priest in the following year.

Thereupon he renounced the composition of secular plays, but he continued to write religious plays, having a monopoly on the authorship of Madrid *autos sacramentales* (two new ones annually) for the rest of his life.

From 1653 to 1657 he was a chaplain in Toledo. In the latter year, he returned to Madrid for good and in 1663 he became a royal chaplain. He was at work on an *auto* when he died in 1681.

According to a list he himself compiled in 1680, Calderón wrote more than 110 *comedias* and more than 70 *autos sacramentales*. (This extant list provides authentications that are sadly lacking for other Siglo de Oro playwrights and also assures us that not much of Calderón's work has been lost.) Many of his plays were published in his own lifetime, in editions of 1636, 1637 (these first two volumes nominally edited by his brother José), 1664 (edited by a friend), 1672 (with a prologue by the author), and 1677 (an edition that he disacknowledged); *comedias* by Calderón also were published in multiauthor anthologies. The first volume of his *autos* appeared in a good edition in 1677. Calderón also wrote texts for *zarzuelas* (two-act musical plays with spoken dialogue; his first one dates from 1648), at least two librettos for fully sung operas[1], some brief skits (*entremeses*), and a fair amount of lyric poetry.

Calderón's *comedias* have been classified in various ways, but it is safe to say that they include religious, historical, amorous-intrigue (*capa y espada*: "cloak-and-sword"), philosophical, mythological, and chivalric plays. A special category closely associated with Calderón is plays about (sexual) honor, in some of which innocent wives are killed by their husbands merely for not being "above suspicion." Interpretation of these plays is divided. Some critics believe that Calderón was on the side of the husbands and attempting to preserve "family values" at a time when Spanish mores were slackening, others believe that he was subtly trying to undermine the outmoded Spanish code of honor by showing what drastic results it could have. Taken as a whole, Calderón's *comedias*, when compared to those of his predecessors, particularly Lope, exhibit tighter plot construction, with no superfluous characters or irrelevant digressions, and with fewer locales for the

---

1. The first of these was *La púrpura de la rosa* (The Purple of the Rose; 1660), on the subject of Venus and Adonis. The original music, by Juan Hidalgo (1612–1685), is lost (whether it was "the first" opera ever mounted in Madrid is a question of definition), but there currently are two complete CD recordings of the music written in 1701 by the Spanish-born Tomás de Torrejón y Velasco (1644–1728) for a performance in Lima ("the first opera produced in Latin America").

action; his poetry is especially fine and *soigné*, and he has a liking for very long speeches, though he also uses rapid-fire half-line exchanges of dialogue to enliven the pace.

Other important Calderón *comedias* other than *La vida es sueño* (this list could be greatly extended) are: *La devoción de la cruz* (Devotion to the Cross; ca. 1625), *El príncipe constante* (The Steadfast Prince; 1629), *El médico de su honra* (The Physician to His Good Name; 1635), *El mágico prodigioso* (The Wonder-Working Magician; 1637), and *El alcalde de Zalamea* (The Mayor of Zalamea; ca. 1640). Among his most magnificent *autos sacramentales* are: *La cena de Baltasar* (Belshazzar's Feast; ca. 1630) and *El gran teatro del mundo* (The Great Theater of the World; ca. 1635, but dated much later by some critics; Calderón alludes to its title—by coincidence?— in *La vida es sueño*, and Hugo von Hofmannsthal emulated the play in his 1923 mystery play *Das Salzburger Grosse Welttheater*).

Calderón's plays remained popular in the early eighteenth century, but were less highly regarded during the Enlightenment. He was idolized again in the Romantic era, especially in Germany, where he was very influential throughout the nineteenth century. At the end of that century, in Spain, the tide turned in favor of Lope's realism, and Calderón's often allegorical, symbolic, and mystical plays were considered stiff and contrived. Today Calderón is recognized as one of the truly great figures in world drama, and his reputation appears to be secure.

Calderón's Play *La vida es sueño*

Calderón's plays are so numerous and varied, and so uniformly high in quality, that it is invidious to choose a single "masterpiece" (several different ones have been named), but it is usual, if not axiomatic, to find *La vida es sueño* called his best, and possibly the best of all Spanish plays. Its fundamental philosophic problem-posing has kept it timely through the years; it had special appeal in the Existentialist and Absurdist theater after the Second World War.

Composition and Publication. There are scattered references to an "earlier version" of the play, about 1630, but a great Calderón scholar places the period of composition between May 1634 (on the basis of strong evidence) and November 1635 (a firm date, that of the official government approval to print it). It first was published as the first item in *Primera parte de comedias de don Pedro Calderón de la*

*Barca, recogidas por don Joseph Calderón de la Barca, su hermano
. . .*, Madrid, 1636, published by María Quiñones, printed by the
booksellers Pedro Coello and Manuel López. In the same year, it was
published "at the Royal and General Hospital of Our Lady of Grace"
in Saragossa, in *Parte treinta de comedias famosas de varios autores.*

Sources. The play is largely imaginative and, though it nominally
takes place in Poland, is not based on history (some editors gratu-
itously place the action in the sixteenth century). Calderón seems to
have derived some personal names from a 1629 work by Enrique
Suárez de Mendoza y Figueroa, titled *Eustorgia y Clorilene, historia
moscovita* (and there *were* real Polish kings named Sigismund, the last
of whom had died as recently as 1632).

The major direct source for *La vida es sueño*, however, was another
play that Calderón himself had written not very long before in collab-
oration with Antonio Coello y Ochoa (1611–1652; also the author of
the very first play anywhere about the loves of Elizabeth and Essex).
This collaborative work was *Yerros de naturaleza y aciertos de la fortuna* (Mistakes of Nature Rectified by Fortune; not published until
1930). In *Yerros*, which has some of the same character names as *La
vida es sueño* (but not corresponding to the analogous people in that
play), an ambitious princess orders her look-alike twin brother to be
killed secretly so that she can reign in his stead, adopting his persona
(it is given out that she has drowned). Her confidant, loyal to the family, imprisons his rightful ruler instead of killing him, even though the
young man, who loves his daughter, has insulted him in a thoughtless
fit of anger. The confidant's son, obsessed with avenging the affront to
his father, unwittingly kills the princess, who has assumed the identity
of the affronter. The prince is brought back to the palace blindfolded
and expresses his amazement at the vicissitudes that have befallen him;
restored to power, he marries the daughter of the man he had insulted.

Thus, the play *Yerros* anticipates the motif of Segismundo's amazement in the palace, and it contains other "pre-echoes" of events and
dialogue in *La vida es sueño*. For instance, in *Yerros* the confidant is
slapped by the prince, whereas in *La vida es sueño* a slap in the face
is cited by Clotaldo (near the end of Act One) as a type of affront from
her ruler that Rosaura should take in stride. Moreover, Segismundo's
defenestration of the punctilious courtier corresponds to an unexe-
cuted threat to do the same uttered by the forceful princess in *Yerros*.
But *La vida es sueño* is immeasurably richer, not merely because it
emphasizes the great themes of dream versus reality and predestina-
tion versus free will, but also because it avoids unusual coincidences

and allows its main character to mature. (One infelicitous aspect of *La vida es sueño*—giving the name of Clorilene to Basilio's late wife as well as to one of his sisters—is probably due to a careless transference of a name from *Yerros*.)[2]

Characters. Segismundo, whom Spanish critics customarily mention in the same breath as Hamlet, is the innocent sufferer, but also the most energetic, and at the same time reflective, person in the play. His female counterpart, not far behind him on all counts, is Rosaura, the other "hybrid" (see the section "Theatricality; Symbols and Images," below), whose scenes with Segismundo progressively serve to humanize him; incidentally, the name she assumes as Estrella's lady-in-waiting, Astraea, is that of the Greco-Roman goddess of justice, who left the earth for heaven when man's Golden Age was over—a fitting name for one seeking restoration of her honor. (The female honor-seeker, and cross-dresser, was a typical figure in Spanish Golden Age drama, but Rosaura is no run-of-the-mill character!)

The couple formed by Astolfo and Estrella (his name is borrowed from that of one of the heroes of Ludovico Ariosto's epic poem *Orlando furioso* of 1532; hers means "star") is much more conventional; they are typical young lovers of Spanish drama. Astolfo's speech is extravagantly flowery (his imagery is never as profound or incisive as Segismundo's), but he can be brave and generous; in her last speech before the battle, Estrella promises to shine as a warrior, but nothing comes of it.

Of the two old men, Clotaldo is somewhat turgid and bumbling, like Polonius in *Hamlet*, but has an even more rounded and decisive part to play; whereas Basilio, in the eyes of Calderón's contemporaries, would be seen to derogate sadly from his royal station by dabbling in astrology, and absolutely to disgrace it by appearing in disguise out of "foolish curiosity," so that it is no jolt to see him lose his throne.

Clarín is in many ways the paragon of *graciosos*—timorous, greedy, self-seeking, sly, amoral, and endlessly punning—but his adventure in Act Three raises his status immeasurably and links him solidly to the overall message of the play.

---

2. These, of course, are merely the direct sources for *La vida es sueño*. It seemed needless here to dwell on the innumerable literary and musical works inspired by the folk motif of the indigent sleeper awakened into a brief moment of glory. An archetypal instance is the story of Abu Hassan in *The Thousand and One Nights*. The outstanding instance in English literature is the adventure of Christopher Sly in the Induction to Shakespeare's *Taming of the Shrew* (before 1594).

The palace "servants" are apparently courtiers of considerable standing, and not mere flunkies.

Theatricality; Symbols and Images. Often branded stodgy, even in the recent past, Calderón actually displays outstanding theatricality. Among the memorable visual treats of *La vida es sueño* is the opening, with the discovery of Segismundo's dungeon (the costumes and props play their part, his animal skins symbolizing his feral nature, and his flickering lamp symbolizing the ray of humanity and hope left to him). Another is the pompous simultaneous entrance of the young lovers, Astolfo escorted by trumpet-blowing and salvo-firing soldiers, and Estrella by beauteous maidens. Rosaura's sword, frequently changing hands and being sheathed and unsheathed, is a striking (phallic) symbol of her family relationships. Also, the audience's ears constantly are regaled with drums, gunshots, fanfares, flourishes, tuckets, sennets, and alarms.

As in Shakespeare, there are frequent self-referential allusions to the theater itself. Clarín jokes about morality plays and window tickets for performances, and boasts that, in his crevice between rocks, he can watch the battle as if it were a show. Segismundo refers to existence as a *gran teatro*, and Basilio laments that the throne of law has become "a grisly theater."

The whole play is a tissue of symbols and metaphors. The light–darkness contrast permeates the entire work, with its innumerable references to lamps, the sun (which becomes eclipsed), the stars, and so on. But perhaps the most distinctive set of symbols in *La vida es sueño* is the network of references to hybrids and monsters, which begins with the opening words *Hipogrifo violento* ("Impetuous hippogriff")[3] and is elaborated on in the rest of Rosaura's first speech. The hippogriff, a combination of horse and griffin, played a prominent part in the above-mentioned epic by Ariosto; here, it not only refers directly to Rosaura's horse, which has bolted, thrown her, and "flown" off a cliff, but also indirectly to the two major "hybrid" characters of the play (who, moreover, are both *violento*), the only-semi-human Segismundo and Rosaura herself, who is not only dressed in male attire but is out on an adventure unsuitable for women in that day and age. The "hybrid" motif reemerges each and every time a

---

3. It's mind-boggling to see that so many translators of the play (including very good ones) have bent over backward, using wordy, diluted paraphrases, to avoid translating the first two words literally (and so have contradicted Calderón's clear intentions). They no doubt wished to make things easier for a modern reader or spectator, but a hippogriff wasn't exactly an everyday sight on the streets of Madrid in 1635, either!

horse is mentioned later on, and also in such passages as Segismundo's first monologue (a fish is an "abortion of algae and slime"), Basilio's narrative (the monster seen in his late wife's dream), and Rosaura's reference to herself as a bisexual monster in her long address to Segismundo in Act Three. (Her key opening speech at the beginning of the play also introduces: [1] the frequently recurring leitmotif of the labyrinth—not only a confusing place, but the home of the bull-man Minotaur, the archetypical hybrid monster—and [2] that of hurling or hurtling downward [*despeñar(se)*], which is echoed by Segismundo's treatment of the second "servant" and by Clarín's wager in Act Three that the prince will do the same thing to Clotaldo.)

To cite only one more noteworthy example of reverberating imagery in the play: Basilio's first speech after the uprising has begun mentions not only a bolting horse (like Rosaura's at the very beginning), but also a boulder that has rolled down a mountain (Rosaura's description of Segismundo's tower in the opening scene).

Another important plot element is that of omens and prophecies. The actual onstage coming-true of the prediction that Basilio will grovel at Segismundo's feet is a feature that has analogies in numerous other Calderón plays. (Sometimes the prophecies are even more oracular, and their coming-true is thus even more of a surprise.)

Poetry. Like Shakespeare's best works, *La vida es sueño* is just as much a poem in dramatic form as a play in verse. Calderón was a poet of the first rank, strongly influenced by the foremost Golden Age lyric poet, (Luis de Argote y) Góngora (1561–1627), with his sophisticated and learned system of metaphors and poetic conceits. (Calderón specialized, for instance, in the accumulation of long metaphors that are swiftly summarized at the very end of the passage, a prime example being the "to a limpid stream, to a fish, a beast, and a bird" at the end of Segismundo's first monologue.)

The following rhyme and stanza schemes (in the order of their first appearance) are used in *La vida es sueño*. (Indentations in the text indicate beginnings of stanzas, beginnings of *romance* passages, and every other line of couplets.)

Silvas pareadas (rhyming couplets, with one 7-syllable and one 11-syllable line).[4] These occur: from the very opening of the play down

---

4. In Spanish verse, the nominal syllable count reflects the reality only when the line ends in a feminine rhyme or assonance. There is actually one syllable less when the rhyme is masculine, and one more in the rare instances when the rhyme word is trisyllabic and stressed on the first syllable.

to Segismundo's monologue; from Rosaura's first entrance in women's clothing through Astolfo's defense of Clotaldo; and in Clarín's description of Rosaura's arrival on horseback in Act Three.

Décimas (stanzas of ten 8-syllable lines each, rhyming ABBAAC-CDDC). These occur: in Segismundo's first monologue; and in the entire last setting of Act Two, back in the prison.

Romance (based on the scheme of medieval narrative ballads, and traditionally used for narratives and "messenger's speeches" in plays, the *romance* consists of an indefinite even number of 8-syllable lines, every second one of which assonates on the same pair of vowels). For example, in the first *romance* passage in the play, the first meeting of Rosaura and Clotaldo, every second line ends in a word with the vowels A and E—*pArtE*, *sobrArEn*, *cobArdEs*, etc. The *romance* is far and away the most extensively used poetic form in *La vida es sueño*. Other *romance* passages are: from Basilio's narrative through the end of Act One; the opening of Act Two down to Segismundo's entrance; the entire portrait sequence with Estrella, Rosaura, and Astolfo; the whole opening of Act Three at the prison; the scene between Rosaura and Segismundo before the battle; and the whole action after Clarín's last appearance through the end of the play.

Quintillas (stanzas of five 8-syllable lines each, rhyming ABBCB or ABABA). They occur from the first entrance of Astolfo and Estrella down to Basilio's narrative.

Redondillas (quatrains of 8-syllable lines, rhyming ABBA). These occur: from Segismundo's first entrance in Act Two down to Rosaura's entrance in female garb; in the casuistic exchange between Rosaura and Clotaldo in Act Three; and in the last sequence in which Clarín figures.

Octavas reales (ottava rima, stanzas of eight 11-syllable lines each, rhyming ABABABCC). They occur in the first Act Three sequence in which Basilio appears, when the inception of the popular uprising is described.

The *Auto Sacramental* of the Same Name. In 1673 (there may have been earlier versions) Calderón wrote an *auto* to which he also gave the title *La vida es sueño*, obviously basing it to a large extent on his earlier great *comedia*, which he thus adapted for more overtly religious purposes (*a lo divino*). In the *auto*, the Four Elements (Earth, Water, Air, and Fire) are in chaotic discord (the world just recently has been created, and Lucifer's rebellion just has taken place). The Three Persons of the Holy Trinity appear and announce that Man will be able to rule and control the Elements. The Power of Darkness, hearing this, seeks Lucifer's aid. Man, dressed in skins, is released from the prison of Nonbeing; Grace accompanies him, carrying a torch. Man, who is given a speech that is very close to Segismundo's first monologue, and who is similarly amazed to find himself acclaimed, pridefully insists on his own free will and freedom of action. Lucifer and Darkness offer him a poisoned apple. Free Will encourages him to pursue sensory delights, while Understanding urges him to use his reason. Becoming vastly conceited, Man hurls Understanding from a height and eats the apple, then falls into a lethargy. The Second Person of the Trinity, Wisdom, promises to save humanity by taking on human nature. When Man awakens, he wonders whether it all has been a dream, but he receives a promise of Redemption. Finally, as befits a Corpus Christi play, each of the Elements supplies some part of what will become the Eucharist. (The *auto* is much more subtle than this very brief summary can indicate.) It is not necessary to imagine that Calderón already had all of these analogies in mind when writing the earlier *comedia* to find an enrichment of it in the words of the *auto sacramental*.

The Nature of This Edition

The translation offered here is absolutely complete, and neither an adaptation nor a paraphrase. It strives to be as accurate and close to the original as possible (though wiser heads have disagreed over the interpretation of certain poetic images and the selection of the English *mot juste* where Spanish words have multiple meanings—not to mention the risk of failing to recognize an obsolescent idiom—so that any claim to perfection would be hubris). Moreover, this new translation is not in paragraph-style prose (which negates the original intention), nor in English verse forms that depart from the Spanish in line length and count (and in other, more serious ways). Instead, without attempting to mimic the original meters and rhymes or assonances—a practice inevitably destructive of accuracy—it conveys the meaning line for line, except where the difference in syntax between the two languages necessitates redistribution of the textual content over two or more lines.

In the Spanish text, reprinted from a good edition, the spelling is modernized and the punctuation is regularized. (This is the practice of most current Spanish editors.)

Unlike some modern Spanish editions and translations, which add

scene numbers whenever a character makes a major entrance or exit
(a nineteenth-century editing practice)[5] and (sometimes infelici-
tously) supply very specific scene locations, this new translation in-
tentionally limits itself (with a very slight amount of regularization) to
the sparse indications in the first edition. It seemed preferable to em-
ulate the fluidity of Calderón's stage, and to let the reader gather the
locations from the dialogue, the way Calderón's audience did.

A few of this edition's footnotes provide explanations that were too
detailed to fit in the Introduction. Others present some of the most
significant variant readings and/or interpretations of the Spanish text,
or analyze some of the Spanish puns that no effort of the translator's
ingenuity was able to render in an English equivalent.

---

5. These artificial scene changes frequently occur in midstanza of poetry, or in the
midst of a long *romance* passage, or otherwise interrupt the poetic structure.

Life Is a Dream

La vida es sueño

Personas

ROSAURA [ROS.], dama
SEGISMUNDO [SEG.], príncipe.
CLOTALDO [CLO.], viejo.
ESTRELLA [EST.], infanta.
SOLDADOS [SOL.].
CLARÍN [CLA.], gracioso.
BASILIO [BAS.], rey.
ASTOLFO [AST.], príncipe.
GUARDAS [GUA.].
MÚSICOS [MUS.].
CRIADOS [CRI.].
DAMAS.
ACOMPAÑAMIENTO DEL REY.

Characters

ROSAURA [ROS.], a noble lady [from Muscovy].

SEGISMUNDO [SEG.], a prince[1] [of Poland].

CLOTALDO [CLO.], an old man [a courtier, Segismundo's jailer].

ESTRELLA [EST.], a princess[1] [of an unspecified country, Basilio's niece].

SOLDIERS [SOL.].

CLARÍN [CLA.], comedian [Rosaura's servant].

BASILIO [BAS.], king [of Poland].

ASTOLFO [AST.], a prince [duke of Muscovy, Basilio's nephew].

GUARDS.[2]

MUSICIANS.

SERVANTS [SER.].

LADIES.

KING'S RETINUE.

[The scene is at or near the royal court of Poland
at an unspecified time.]

---

1. Strictly, a *príncipe* is a crown prince, whereas an *infante* (female: *infanta*) is a younger child of the king, not expected to reign after him.   2. Characters for whom no abbreviation is supplied have no speaking parts, except where "ALL," "VOICES WITHIN," or the like is indicated.

3

Jornada primera

Sale en lo alto de un monte ROSAURA *en hábito de hombre, de camino, y en representando los primeros versos va bajando.*

ROS.:   Hipogrifo violento,
que corriste parejas con el viento,
   ¿dónde, rayo sin llama,
pájaro sin matiz, pez sin escama,
   y bruto sin instinto
natural, al confuso laberinto
   de esas desnudas peñas
te desbocas, te arrastras y despeñas?
   Quédate en este monte,
donde tengan los brutos su Faetonte;
   que yo, sin más camino
que el que me dan las leyes del destino,
   ciega y desesperada,
bajaré la cabeza enmarañada
   de este monte eminente
que arruga al sol el ceño de la frente.
   Mal, Polonia, recibes
a un extranjero, pues con sangre escribes
   su entrada en tus arenas,
y apenas llega, cuando llega a penas.
   Bien mi suerte lo dice;
mas ¿dónde halló piedad un infelice?

Sale CLARÍN, *gracioso.*

4

Act One

High on a mountain ROSAURA *enters dressed like a male wayfarer, and she descends as she speaks her first lines.*[1]

ROS.:   Impetuous hippogriff
that matched the wind in speed,
    flash without flame,
bird without bright plumage, fish without scales,
    and beast without natural
instincts: where, in the confused labyrinth
    of these bare rocks,
are you bolting, hugging the ground, and hurtling down?
    Remain on this mountain,
so that the beasts can have their Phaethon[2] here;
    for I, with no more distinct path
than the one which the laws of destiny afford me,
    a woman blinded by despair,
shall descend the tangled head
    of this lofty mountain,
which furrows its brow in a scowl at the sun.[3]
    Poland, you give an ill welcome
to a foreigner, since you mark his entrance
    on your sands with blood,
and hardly has he come when he comes into hardship.
    My fate states this plainly,
but where has an unhappy person ever found mercy?

Enter CLARÍN, *the comic.*

---

1. See the Introduction concerning the original staging of this scene and the significance of Rosaura's first words. 2. The son of the sun god who misappropriated his father's chariot and caused disaster when he couldn't control the horses. 3. Another text reads *abrasa* for *arruga*, which would make the line mean: "which burns its knitted brow in the sunshine."

CLA.:   Di dos, y no me dejes
            en la posada a mí cuando te quejes;
            que si dos hemos sido
            los que de nuestra patria hemos salido
            a probar aventuras;
            dos los que, entre desdichas y locuras,
            aquí habemos llegado,
            y dos los que del monte hemos rodado,
            ¿no es razón que yo sienta
            meterme en el pesar, y no en la cuenta?
ROS.:   No quise darte parte
            en mis quejas, Clarín, por no quitarte,
            llorando tu desvelo,
            el derecho que tienes al consuelo;
            que tanto gusto había
            en quejarse, un filósofo decía,
            que, a trueco de quejarse,
            habían las desdichas de buscarse.
CLA.:   El filósofo era
            un borracho barbón; ¡oh, quién le diera
            más de mil bofetadas!
            Quejárase después de muy bien dadas.
            Mas, ¿qué haremos, señora,
            a pie, solos, perdidos y a esta hora,
            en un desierto monte
            cuando se parte el sol a otro horizonte?
ROS.:   ¿Quién ha visto sucesos tan extraños?
            Mas si la vista no padece engaños
            que hace la fantasía,
            a la medrosa luz que aún tiene el día
            me parece que veo
            un edificio.
CLA.:   O miente mi deseo
            o termino las señas.
ROS.:   Rústico nace entre desnudas peñas
            un palacio tan breve,
            que el sol apenas a mirar se atreve.
            Con tan rudo artificio
            la arquitectura está de su edificio,
            que parece, a las plantas
            de tantas rocas y de peñas tantas

CLA.:   Say "two unhappy people," and don't leave *me*
         "back at the inn" when you complain;
            because, if there were two of us
         who left our homeland
            in search of adventures,
         two of us who arrived here
            amid misfortunes and madness,
         and two of us who rolled down the mountain,
            isn't it right for me to resent
         being added to the anguish and not to the account?

ROS.:   I refrained from giving you a share
         in my laments, Clarín, so as not to deprive you,
            by bemoaning your troubles,
         of your own right to consolation;
            because a philosopher once said
         there was such pleasure in lamenting
            that, in exchange for a good cry,
         people should actually seek misfortunes.

CLA.:   That philosopher was
         a drunken old goat! Oh, I'd like to give him
            more than a thousand slaps in the face!
         Then he could complain about my accurate aim!
            But, my lady, what will we do
         on foot, alone, lost, at this time of day,
            on a deserted mountain
         when the sun is leaving for another horizon?

ROS.:   Who has ever seen such strange events?
         But, if my eyes aren't suffering delusions
            created by my imagination,
         in the timorous light that the day still holds
            I seem to see
         a building.

CLA.:   Either my wishes are telling me lies,
            or I can make out the trace of it, too.

ROS.:   Amid the bare rocks there rises a rustic
            palace so small
         that it scarcely dares to behold the sun.
            Of such coarse workmanship
         is the architecture of its structure
            that, at the foot
         of so many crags and rocks

que al sol tocan la lumbre,
peñasco que ha rodado de la cumbre.

CLA.: Vámonos acercando,
que éste es mucho mirar, señora, cuando
es mejor que la gente
que habita en ella, generosamente
nos admita.

ROS. La puerta
(mejor diré funesta boca) abierta
está, y desde su centro
nace la noche, pues la engendra dentro.

Suena ruido de cadenas.

CLA.: ¡Qué es lo que escucho, cielo!
ROS.: Inmóvil bulto soy de fuego y hielo.
CLA.: Cadenita hay que suena,
mátenme, si no es galeote en pena;
bien mi temor lo dice.

Dentro SEGISMUNDO.

SEG.: ¡Ay, mísero de mí, y ay, infelice!
ROS.: ¡Qué triste voz escucho!
Con nuevas penas y tormentos lucho.
CLA.: Yo con nuevos temores.
ROS.: ¡Clarín!
CLA.: ¡Señora!
ROS.: Huyamos los rigores
de esta encantada torre.
CLA.: Yo aún no tengo
ánimo de huir, cuando a eso vengo.
ROS.: ¿No es breve luz aquella
caduca exhalación, pálida estrella,
que en trémulos desmayos,
pulsando ardores y latiendo rayos,
hace más tenebrosa
la obscura habitación con luz dudosa?
Sí, pues a sus reflejos
puedo determinar (aunque de lejos)
una prisión obscura,
que es de un vivo cadáver sepultura,
y porque más me asombre,

that reach up into the bright sun, it resembles
a boulder that has rolled down from the summit.

CLA.:   Let's go closer to it,
my lady; we've been just looking at it too long, when
   it would be better if the people
who live in it were to let us in
   hospitably.

ROS.:   The door
(or should I say "the grim maw"?) is
   open, and from its interior
emerges the night, which is engendered within it.

A noise of chains is heard.

CLA.:   What's that I hear?! Heavens!
ROS.:   I've turned into a motionless figure of fire and ice.
CLA.:   There's a little chain rattling;
may I be killed if it isn't a galley slave's spirit in torment!
My fear clearly tells me so.

SEGISMUNDO *is heard from within.*

SEG.:   Ah, woe is me! Ah, how wretched I am!
ROS.:   What a sad cry I hear!
I struggle with new pains and torments.
CLA.:   And I with new fears.
ROS.:   Clarín!
CLA.:   My lady?
ROS.:   Let us flee the harshness
of this enchanted tower!
CLA.:   I don't yet have
enough courage to run away when I try to.
ROS.:   Isn't it a small lamp, that
feeble glare, that pallid star,
   which, in fitful swoons,
pulsating beams, and throbbing flashes,
   makes the gloomy dwelling
darker yet with its dubious light?
   Yes, because by its reflections
I can discern (although from afar)
   a dark dungeon,
which is the tomb of a living corpse;
   and, to add to my awe,

en el traje de fiera yace un hombre
de prisiones cargado
y sólo de la luz acompañado.
    Pues huir no podemos,
desde aquí sus desdichas escuchemos;
    sepamos lo que dice.

Descúbrese SEGISMUNDO *con una cadena y la luz,*
vestido de pieles.

SEG.:   ¡Ay, mísero de mí, y ay, infelice!
    Apurar, cielos, pretendo,
ya que me tratáis así
qué delito cometí
contra vosotros, naciendo;
aunque si nací, ya entiendo
qué delito he cometido:
bastante causa ha tenido
vuestra justicia y rigor,
pues el delito mayor
del hombre es haber nacido.
    Sólo quisiera saber
para apurar mis desvelos
(dejando a una parte, cielos,
el delito de nacer),
qué más os pude ofender
para castigarme más.
¿No nacieron los demás?
Pues si los demás nacieron,
¿qué privilegios tuvieron
que yo no gocé jamás?
    Nace el ave, y con las galas
que le dan belleza suma,
apenas es flor de pluma
o ramillete con alas,
cuando las etéreas salas
corta con velocidad,
negándose a la piedad
del nido que deja en calma;
¿y teniendo yo más alma,
tengo menos libertad?
    Nace el bruto, y con la piel

dressed like a wild beast there lies a man
loaded with shackles
and with only the lamp for company.
Since we cannot flee,
let's listen to his misfortune from where we stand;
let's learn what he says.

SEGISMUNDO *is discovered with a chain and the lamp;*
he is dressed in animal skins.

SEG.:   Ah, woe is me! Ah, how wretched I am!
Heavens, I seek to inquire—
since you treat me this way—
what crime I committed
against you when I was born;
though, seeing that I was born, I already realize
what crime I have committed:
there was sufficient reason for
your justice and severity,
since the greatest crime
of man is being born.
I would merely like to know,
in order to determine the cause of my woes
(setting apart, O heavens,
the crime of being born),
in what other way I could have offended you
to deserve additional punishment.
Wasn't everyone else born, too?
Well, then, if everyone else was born,
what special favors were they granted
which I have never enjoyed?
The bird is born, and in the finery
that gives it supreme beauty,
no sooner does it become a feathered flower,
or a winged posy,
than it swiftly cuts its way
through the halls of the sky,
abandoning the family relations
of its nest, which it leaves in repose.
And I, who have more soul,
have less liberty?
The beast is born, and with its coat

que dibujan manchas bellas,
apenas signo es de estrellas
(gracias al docto pincel),
cuando atrevida y cruel
la humana necesidad
le enseña a tener crueldad,
monstruo de su laberinto;
¿y yo, con mejor instinto,
tengo menos libertad?
Nace el pez, que no respira,
aborto de ovas y lamas,
y apenas, bajel de escamas,
sobre las ondas se mira,
cuando a todas partes gira,
midiendo la inmensidad
de tanta capacidad
como le da el centro frío;
¿y yo, con más albedrío,
tengo menos libertad?
Nace el arroyo, culebra
que entre flores se desata,
y apenas, sierpe de plata,
entre las flores se quiebra,
cuando músico celebra
de las flores la piedad,
que le dan la majestad
del campo abierto a su huida;
¿y teniendo yo más vida
tengo menos libertad?
En llegando a esta pasión,
un volcán, un Etna hecho,
quisiera sacar del pecho
pedazos del corazón.
¿Qué ley, justicia o razón,
negar a los hombres sabe
privilegio tan suave,
excepción tan principal,
que Dios le ha dado a un cristal,

patterned with beautiful spots,
no sooner is it starred like a constellation
(thanks to Nature's skilled brush)
than the bold and cruel
needs of mankind[4]
teach it to become cruel in turn,
a monster in its own labyrinth.
And I, with finer instincts,
have less liberty?
    The fish is born, which doesn't breathe,
an abortion of algae[5] and slime,
and no sooner does it find itself on the waves,
like a boat of scales,
than it turns in every direction,
measuring the immensity
of all the space
that its cold element gives it.
And I, with more free will,
have less liberty?
    The stream is born, a snake
winding amid flowers,
and, like a silver serpent, no sooner
does it twist through the flowers
than it musically acclaims
the kindness of the flowers,
which lend it the majesty
of the open fields as it flees past.
And I, who have more life,
have less liberty?
    When I reach this pitch of emotion,
I become a volcano, an Etna,
and I'd like to pull pieces
of my heart out of my breast.
What law, justice, or philosophy
is able to deny men
so sweet a privilege,
so fundamental an exemption,
which God has granted to a limpid stream,

---

4. In another interpretation, *humana* is taken to mean [the animal's own] "natural" [needs], and some editors even emend it to *huraña* ("surly").   5. Or: "roe."

	a un pez, a un bruto y a un ave?

Ros.:   Temor y piedad en mí
sus razones han causado.

Seg.:   ¿Quién mis voces ha escuchado?
¿Es Clotaldo?

Cla.:   Di que sí.

Ros.:   No es sino un triste (¡ay de mí!)
que en estas bóvedas frías
oyó tus melancolías.

                                    Asela.

Seg.:   Pues la muerte te daré,
porque no sepas que sé
que sabes flaquezas mías.
   Sólo porque me has oído,
entre mis membrudos brazos
te tengo de hacer pedazos.

Cla.:   Yo soy sordo, y no he podido
escucharte.

Ros.:   Si has nacido
humano, baste el postrarme
a tus pies para librarme.

Seg.:   Tu voz pudo enternecerme,
tu presencia suspenderme,
y tu respeto turbarme.
   ¿Quién eres? que aunque yo aquí
tan poco del mundo sé,
que cuna y sepulcro fue
esta torre para mí;
y aunque desde que nací
(si esto es nacer) sólo advierto
este rústico desierto
donde miserable vivo,
siendo un esqueleto vivo,
siendo un animado muerto;
   y aunque nunca vi ni hablé
sino a un hombre solamente
que aquí mis desdichas siente,
por quien las noticias sé
de cielo y tierra; y aunque
aquí, porque más te asombres

	to a fish, a beast, and a bird?
Ros.:	His words have aroused fear and pity in me.
Seg.:	Who has been listening to my cries? Is it Clotaldo?
Cla.:	Say that it is!
Ros.:	No, it's a sad man (woe is me!) who in these chilly vaults has overheard your melancholy.

SEGISMUNDO *seizes* ROSAURA.

Seg.:	In that case, I shall put you to death, to prevent your knowing that I know that you know my weakness.

Seg.:   In that case, I shall put you to death,
        to prevent your knowing that I know
        that you know my weakness.
            Merely because you overheard me,
        with my brawny arms
        I must tear you to shreds.
Cla.:   As for me, I'm deaf, and I wasn't able
        to listen to you.
Ros.:   If you were born
        human, my prostrating myself at your feet
        should be enough for you to set me free.
Seg.:   Your voice has had the power to soften me,
        your presence to interrupt me,
        and respect for you to confuse me.
            Who are you? Because, even though
        I know so little of the world here,
        since for me this tower
        has been my cradle and my grave;
        and, even though, ever since my birth
        (if you can call it birth) the only thing I have beheld
        is this rustic wilderness
        in which I live wretchedly,
        like a living skeleton,
        like an animated corpse;
            and, even though I have never seen nor spoken to
        any man but one,
        who listens to my misfortunes here,
        and from whom I have gathered all my knowledge
        about heaven and earth; and, even though
        here—this will surprise you more

y monstruo humano me nombres,
entre asombros y quimeras,
soy un hombre de las fieras
y una fiera de los hombres.
    Y aunque en desdichas tan graves
la política he estudiado,
de los brutos enseñado,
advertido de las aves;
y de los astros suaves
los círculos he medido:
tú sólo, tú has suspendido
la pasión a mis enojos,
la suspensión a mis ojos,
la admiración al oído.
    Con cada vez que te veo
nueva admiración me das,
y cuando te miro más,
aún más mirarte deseo.
Ojos hidrópicos creo
que mis ojos deben ser,
pues cuando es muerte el beber
beben más, y de esta suerte,
viendo que el ver me da muerte
estoy muriendo por ver.
    Pero véate yo y muera,
que no sé, rendido ya,
si el verte muerte me da
el no verte qué me diera.
Fuera más que muerte fiera,
ira, rabia y dolor fuerte;
fuera muerte, de esta suerte
su rigor he ponderado,
pues dar vida a un desdichado
es dar a un dichoso muerte.

ROS.:   Con asombro de mirarte,
con admiración de oírte,
ni sé qué pueda decirte,
ni qué pueda preguntarte.

and make you call me a human monster—
amid my fears and wild imaginings
I am a man among beasts
and a beast among men;
    and, even though in such weighty misfortunes
I have studied political science,
instructed by the beasts,
informed by the birds,
and have measured the orbits
of the gentle heavenly bodies:
you alone have interrupted
my emotional response to my troubles,
amazing my eyes
and thrilling my ears.
    Each time I look at you,
you fill me with new wonderment,
and the more I gaze on you
the more I long to do so.
I think my eyes must be
morbidly thirsty,
because, when drinking is death,
they drink all the more, and to this effect:
seeing that seeing gives me death,
I am dying to see.
    But let me see you and die,
because, by now overcome, I don't know—
since seeing you gives me death—
what not seeing you would give me.
It would be something fiercer than death,
anger, frenzy, and sharp pain;
it would be death[6]—for I have calculated
its severity in this way—
because giving life to an unfortunate man
is like giving death to a fortunate one.

Ros.:   Awe-struck at seeing you,
astonished at hearing you,
I don't know what I can say to you,
or what I can ask you.

---

6. Some editors accept the emendation *vida* ("life") instead of *muerte* ("death") in this line.

Sólo diré que a esta parte
hoy el cielo me ha guiado
para haberme consolado,
si consuelo puede ser
del que es desdichado, ver
a otro que es más desdichado.
   Cuentan de un sabio, que un día
tan pobre y mísero estaba,
que sólo se sustentaba
de unas yerbas que cogía.
¿Habrá otro, entre sí decía
más pobre y triste que yo?
Y cuando el rostro volvió,
halló la respuesta, viendo
que iba otro sabio cogiendo
las hojas que él arrojó.
   Quejoso de la fortuna
yo en este mundo vivía
y cuando entre mí decía:
¿habrá otra persona alguna
de suerte más importuna?
piadoso me has respondido,
pues volviendo en mi sentido
hallo que las penas mías
para hacerlas tú alegrías
las hubieras recogido.
   Y por si acaso, mis penas
pueden aliviarte en parte,
óyelas atento, y toma
las que de ellas me sobraren.
Yo soy . . .

Dentro, CLOTALDO.

CLO.:   ¡Guardas desta torre
que, dormidas o cobardes,
disteis paso a dos personas
que han quebrantado la cárcel!

ROS.: ¡Nueva confusión padezco!

SEG.: Este es Clotaldo, mi alcaide:
aún no acaban mis desdichas.

CLO.: ¡Acudid, y vigilantes,
                               (*Dentro*)

I'll only say that heaven
has guided me here today
to give me consolation,
if it can be consolation
to an unfortunate man to see
another more unfortunate.
      The tale is told of a wise man who once
was so poor and indigent
that his sole nourishment
was a few herbs that he picked.
"Can there be another man," he said to himself,
"poorer and sadder than I?"
And when he turned his face,
he found the answer, beholding
another wise man who was gathering
the leaves that he had discarded.
      I was living in this world
lamenting my fortune,
and when I asked myself
whether there was anyone else
with a more troublous fate,
you kindly gave me the answer,
because, on due consideration,
I find that you would have gathered
my sorrows
to turn them into happiness for yourself.
      And if by chance my sorrows
can soothe you to some extent,
listen to them closely and take
any of them that are too many for me.
I am . . .

CLOTALDO is heard from within.

CLO.:   This way, you tower guards,
            who either from drowsiness or cowardice
            have let two people get by
            and enter the secret prison!
ROS.:   I'm upset all over again!
SEG.:   That's Clotaldo, my jailer:
            my misfortunes are not yet at an end.
CLO. (*within*):   Come running, and with vigilance,

	sin que puedan defenderse,
	o prendeldes, o mataldes!

TODOS: ¡Traición!   (*Dentro*)

CLA.:   Guardas desta torre,
que entrar aquí nos dejasteis,
pues que nos dais a escoger.
el prendernos es más fácil.

Sale CLOTALDO *con escopeta, y* SOLDADOS,
todos con los rostros cubiertos.

CLO.: Todos os cubrid los rostros,
que es diligencia importante,
mientras estamos aquí,
que no nos conozca nadie.

CLA.: ¿Enmascaraditos hay?

CLO.: Oh, vosotros, que, ignorantes,
de aqueste vedado sitio
coto y término pasasteis
contra el decreto del rey
que manda que no ose nadie
examinar el prodigio
que entre estos peñascos yace:
rendid las armas y vidas,
o aquesta pistola, áspid
de metal, escupirá
el veneno penetrante
de dos balas, cuyo fuego
será escándalo del aire.

SEG.: Primero, tirano dueño,
que los ofendas y agravies,
será mi vida despojo
de estos lazos miserables,
pues en ellos, vive Dios,
tengo de despedazarme
con las manos, con los dientes,
entre aquestas peñas, antes
que su desdicha consienta
y que llore sus ultrajes.

CLO.: Si sabes que tus desdichas,
Segismundo, son tan grandes,

not allowing them to defend themselves,
either seize them or kill them!

ALL (*within*):   Treason!

CLA.:   Guards of this tower,
who allowed us to enter here,
since you give us our choice,
seizing us is easier.

Enter CLOTALDO *with a gun, and* SOLDIERS,
all with their faces covered.

CLO.:   All of you cover your faces—
it's an important precaution—
as long as we're in here,
so no one can recognize us.

CLA.:   Are they masqueraders?

CLO.:   You who in your ignorance
have passed the bounds and limits
of this forbidden place
in violation of the royal decree
which orders that no one venture
to examine the marvel
that dwells amid these boulders:
surrender your weapons and lives,
or this pistol, a metal
viper, will spit
the penetrating venom
of two bullets, whose fire
will cause an uproar in the air.

SEG.:   Tyrannical master, before
you insult and injure them,
my life will be the spoil
of these unhappy bonds,
because, as God lives, in them
I shall tear myself apart
with my hands, with my teeth,
amid these rocks, before
I consent to their misfortune
and bewail outrages committed against them.

CLO.:   Segismundo, if you know
that your misfortunes are so great

que antes de nacer moriste
por ley del cielo; si sabes
que aquestas prisiones son
de tus furias arrogantes
un freno que las detenga,
y una rienda que las pare,
¿por qué blasonas? La puerta
cerrad de esa estrecha cárcel;
escondelde en ella.

Ciérranle la puerta y dice dentro:

SEG.:   ¡Ah, cielos!
¡Qué bien hacéis en quitarme
la libertad!, porque fuera
contra vosotros gigante
que, para quebrar al sol
esos vidrios y cristales,
sobre cimientos de piedra
pusiera montes de jaspe.

CLO.:   Quizá, porque no los pongas
hoy padeces tantos males.

ROS.:   Ya que vi que la soberbia
te ofendió tanto, ignorante
fuera en no pedirte humilde
vida que a tus plantas yace.
Muévate en mí la piedad,
que será rigor notable
que no hallen favor en ti
ni soberbias ni humildades.

CLA.:   Y si humildad y soberbia
no te obligan, personajes
que han movido y removido
mil autos sacramentales,
yo, ni humilde ni soberbio,
sino entre las dos mitades
entreverado, te pido
que nos remedies y ampares.

CLO.   ¡Hola!

SOL.:   ¡Señor!

CLO.:   A los dos
quitad las armas, y ataldes

that you died before you were born
because of a heavenly law; if you know
that these shackles are
a bridle to your arrogant
fury to keep it in check,
and reins to call it to a halt,
why do you brag? Guards, lock
the door to this cramped prison;
hide him within it.

They lock the door, and he calls from within:

SEG.:   Oh, heaven!
How right you are to deprive me
of freedom! Because I would be
a Titan attacking you,
and in order to smash those
crystals and glasses of the sun,
I would pile up mountains of jasper
atop foundations of stone.

CLO.:   Perhaps it is to prevent you from piling them up
that you undergo so many troubles today.

ROS.:   Now that I've seen that my pride
offended you so, I'd be
a fool not to ask you humbly
for my life, which lies at your feet.
Let pity for me move you,
for it would be exceptional severity
if neither pride nor humility
found favor with you.

CLA.:   And if you aren't under obligation to Humility
and Pride, characters
who have time and again been the motive force
in a thousand morality plays,
then I, neither humble nor proud,
but a mix
of the two, ask you
to aid us and protect us.

CLO.:   You there!

SOL.:   My lord!

CLO.:   Take away
the weapons from both of them, and bind

los ojos, porque no vean
cómo ni de dónde salen.

Ros.: Mi espada es ésta, que a ti
solamente ha de entregarse,
porque, al fin, de todos eres
el principal y no sabe
rendirse a menos valor.

CLA.: La mía es tal que puede darse
al más ruin: tomalda vos.

Ros.: Y si he de morir, dejarte
quiero, en fe de esta piedad,
prenda que pudo estimarse
por el dueño que algún día
se la ciñó; que la guardes
te encargo, porque aunque yo
no sé qué secreto alcance,
sé que esta dorada espada
encierra misterios grandes,
pues sólo fiado en ella
vengo a Polonia a vengarme
de un agravio.

CLO.: ¡Santos cielos!
¿Qué es esto? Ya son más graves
mis penas y confusiones,
mis ansias y mis pesares.
¿Quién te la dio?

Ros. Una mujer.

CLO.: ¿Cómo se llama?

Ros.: Que calle
su nombre es fuerza.

CLO.: ¿De qué
infieres ahora o sabes
que hay secreto en esta espada?

Ros.: Quien me la dio, dijo: "Parte
a Polonia, y solicita
con ingenio, estudio o arte,
que te vean esa espada
los nobles y principales;
que yo sé que alguno dellos
te favorezca y ampare";
que, por si acaso era muerto,

their eyes so they can't see
what way, or from where, they leave.

ROS.:   This is my sword, which to you
alone can be handed over,
because, after all, among all here you are
the leader, and it is unable
to submit to one of less merit.

CLA.:   Mine is such that it can be given
to the lowest man of all: you soldiers take it!

ROS.:   And, if I am to die, I wish
to leave with you, to attest to your compassion,
an object which deserves esteem
for the owner who once
girded it on; I enjoin you
to keep it safely, because, even though I
don't know what secret it involves,
I know that this gilded sword
encloses great mysteries,
since, relying on it alone,
I have come to Poland to avenge myself
for an affront.

CLO.:   Holy God!
What's this? Now I feel even greater
trouble and confusion,
anxiety and worry.
Who gave it to you?

ROS.:   A woman.

CLO.:   What is her name?

ROS.:   I am compelled
to conceal her name.

CLO.:   What
makes you now infer or know
that there's a secret in this sword?

ROS.:   She who gave it to me said: "Leave
for Poland, and make it your business,
through planning, diligence, or craft,
that you are seen with this sword
by the nobility and eminent men;
because I know that one of them
will become your patron and protector."
In case he was dead,

no quiso entonces nombrarle.

CLO.:   ¡Válgame el cielo! ¿qué escucho?
Aún no sé determinarme
si tales sucesos son
ilusiones o verdades.
Esta espada es la que yo
dejé a la hermosa Violante
por señas que el que ceñida
la trajera, había de hallarme
amoroso como hijo
y piadoso como padre.
Pues ¿qué he de hacer (¡ay de mí!)
en confusión semejante,
si quien la trae por favor,
para su muerte la trae,
pues que sentenciado a muerte
llega a mis pies? ¡Qué notable
confusión! ¡Qué triste hado!
¡Qué suerte tan inconstante!
Este es mi hijo, y las señas
dicen bien con las señales
del corazón, que por verle
llama al pecho, y en él bate
las alas, y no pudiendo
romper los candados, hace
lo que aquel que está encerrado
y oyendo ruido en la calle
se asoma por la ventana.
Y él así, como no sabe
lo que pasa, y oye el ruido,
va a los ojos a asomarse,
que son ventanas del pecho
por donde en lágrimas sale.
¿Qué he de hacer? ¡Válgame el cielo!
¿Qué he de hacer? Porque llevarle
al rey, es llevarle (¡ay triste!)
a morir. Pues ocultarle
al rey no puedo, conforme
a la ley del homenaje.
De una parte el amor propio,
y la lealtad de otra parte,

she refused to name him at the time.

CLO.: Heaven help me! What's this I hear?
I still can't decide
whether what's happening is
an illusion or reality.
This sword is the one that I
left with beautiful Violante
as a token that the man who bore it
girded to his waist would find me
as a loving son
finds an affectionate father.
So, what am I to do (woe is me!)
in a dilemma like this,
if the man who wears it for his benefit
is actually wearing it for his death,
seeing that he has surrendered to me
under sentence of death! What a singular
dilemma! What a sad fate!
What a changeable fortune!
This man is my son, and his appearance
corresponds with the signals
of my heart, which cries out
in my breast to see him, and flutters
its wings there, and, unable
to break the padlocks, behaves
like a man who's locked in
and, hearing an uproar in the street,
looks out the window.
And thus my heart, not knowing
what's happening, but hearing the uproar,
goes to look out of my eyes,
which are the windows of the breast
through which it emerges in tears.
What am I to do? Heaven help me!
What am I to do? Because to take him
to the king is to take him (woe is me!)
to his death. But I can't
hide him from the king, since I must obey
the laws of fealty.
Self-love on the one side,
and loyalty on the other,

rinden. Pero, ¿qué dudo?
:altad del rey ¿no es antes
que la vida y que el honor?
Pues ella viva y él falte.
Fuera de que, si ahora atiendo
a que dijo que a vengarse
viene de un agravio, hombre
que está agraviado es infame.
¡No es mi hijo, no es mi hijo
ni tiene mi noble sangre!
Pero si ya ha sucedido
un peligro, de quien nadie
se libró, porque el honor
es de materia tan fácil
que con una acción se quiebra
o se mancha con un aire,
¿qué más puede hacer, qué más,
el que es noble, de su parte,
que a costa de tantos riesgos
haber venido a buscarle?
¡Mi hijo es, mi sangre tiene,
pues tiene valor tan grande!
Y así entre una y otra duda
el medio más importante
es irme al rey y decirle
que es mi hijo, y que le mate.
Quizá la misma piedad
de mi honor podrá obligarle
y si le merezco vivo,
yo le ayudaré a vengarse
de su agravio; mas si el rey,
en sus rigores constante
le da muerte, morirá
sin saber que soy su padre.
Venid conmigo, extranjeros.
No temáis, no, de que os falte
compañía en las desdichas;
pues en duda semejante

overwhelm me. But, why do I hesitate?
Doesn't loyalty to the king come before
life and honor?[7]
Then, let loyalty live and honor fail!
Besides that, if I now pay heed
to the fact that he said he had come
to take revenge for an affront, a man
who has been affronted is base.
He isn't my son, he isn't my son
and doesn't bear my noble blood!
But if it was some
critical situation of the sort that no one
can avoid, because honor
is of such brittle stuff
that it is broken with a gesture
or besmirched by a puff of air,
what more can he do, what more,
on his part, as a nobleman,
than to come in quest of his honor
at the cost of so many risks?
He *is* my son, he bears my blood,
since he possesses such great merit!
And so, between one hesitation and another,
the most imperative course
is to go to the king and tell him
that the man is my son, and that he should kill him.
Perhaps the very pity the king feels
for my honor will place him under an obligation,
and if my merits save this man's life,
I'll help him take revenge
for his affront; but if the king,
unbending in his severity,
puts him to death, he will die
without knowing I'm his father.
Come with me, strangers.
Have no fear, none, that you will lack
for company in your misfortunes;
for in such uncertainty

---

7. At least one Spanish editor is convinced that the last word in this line has to be *amor* ("love") rather than *honor*.

de vivir o de morir,
no sé cuáles son más grandes.   (*Vanse.*)

Sale por una parte ASTOLFO *con acompañamiento de soldados,
y por otra* ESTRELLA *con damas. Suena música.*

AST.:   Bien, al ver los excelentes
rayos, que fueron cometas,
mezclan salvas diferentes
las cajas y las trompetas,
los pájaros y las fuentes;
      siendo con música igual,
y con maravilla suma,
a tu vista celestial
unos, clarines de pluma,
y otras, aves de metal;
      y así os saludan, señora,
como a su reina, las balas,
los pájaros como a Aurora,
las trompetas como a Palas,
y las flores como a Flora;
      porque sois, burlando el día
que ya la noche destierra,
Aurora en el alegría,
Flora en paz, Palas en guerra,
y reina en el alma mía.

EST.:   Si la voz se ha de medir
con las acciones humanas
mal habéis hecho en decir
finezas tan cortesanas
donde os pueda desmentir
      todo ese marcial trofeo
con quien ya atrevida lucho;
pues no dicen, según creo,
las lisonjas que os escucho
con los rigores que veo.
      Y advertid que es baja acción,
que sólo a una fiera toca,
madre de engaño y traición,
el halagar con la boca

over living and dying,
I don't know whose misfortunes are greater.   (*All exit.*)

ASTOLFO *enters from one side, accompanied by soldiers,*
and ESTRELLA *from the other, with ladies-in-waiting. Music plays.*

AST.:   It is fitting, at the sight of your outstanding
beams of light, which were once comets,
that various salvos are intermingled
by the drums and trumpets,
and the birds and fountains;
    since, with equal music
and supreme wondrousness,
upon viewing your heavenly presence,
the birds are feathered clarions
and the trumpets are metallic birds;
    and thus, my lady, you are saluted
by the bullets as their queen,
by the birds as the Dawn,
by the trumpets as Pallas Athena,[8]
and by the flowers as Flora;[9]
    because, mocking the day
which night is now banishing, you are
Dawn in gladness,
Flora in peace, Pallas in war,
and queen in my soul.

EST.:   If words must be pitted
against man's deeds,
you have done wrong to utter
such courtly compliments
when you can be given the lie
    by all this martial pomp,
against which I now boldly struggle;
because, as I believe, the flattery
I hear from you doesn't suit
the grimness that I see.
    And take note that it's a base deed,
one worthy only of a wild animal,
mother of deceit and treachery,
to throw bouquets to a woman with your lips

---

8. A martial goddess.   9. The goddess of flowers.

y matar con la intención.

AST.:   Muy mal informada estáis,
Estrella, pues que la fe
de mis finezas dudáis,
y os suplico que me oigáis
la causa, a ver si la sé.
     Falleció Eustorgio tercero,
rey de Polonia, quedó
Basilio por heredero,
y dos hijas, de quien yo
y vos nacimos. No quiero
     cansar con lo que no tiene
lugar aquí. Clorilene,
vuestra madre y mi señora,
que en mejor imperio ahora
dosel de luceros tiene,
     fue la mayor de quien vos
sois hija; fue la segunda,
madre y tía de los dos,
la gallarda Recisunda,
que guarde mil años Dios.
     Casó en Moscovia, de quien
nací yo. Volver ahora
al otro principio es bien.
Basilio, que ya, señora,
se rinde al común desdén
     del tiempo, más inclinado
a los estudios, que dado
a mujeres, enviudó
sin hijos, y vos y yo
aspiramos a este Estado.
     Vos alegáis que habéis sido
hija de hermana mayor;
yo, que varón he nacido,
y aunque de hermana menor,
os debo ser preferido.
     Vuestra intención y la mía
a nuestro tío contamos;
él respondió que quería
componernos, y aplazamos
este puesto y este día.

and to kill her in your secret thoughts.
AST.:   You're very badly informed,
Estrella, if you doubt
the sincerity of my compliments,
and I beseech you to hear my explanation
of the reason, to see if I know it.
      Eustorgio the Third, king
of Poland, died, leaving
Basilio as heir,
as well as two daughters, one your mother
and one mine. I don't wish
      to tire you out with details that are
irrelevant here. Clorilene,
your mother and my lady aunt,
who now in a better realm
enjoys a canopy of stars,
      was the elder daughter, and you
are hers; Eustorgio's younger daughter,
my mother and your aunt,
is the elegant Recisunda
(may God keep her for a thousand years!).
      She wed in Muscovy, and gave
birth to me. It is now fitting
to return to the beginning again.
Basilio, who by now, my lady,
is yielding to the universal mockery
      of Time, and is more inclined
to study than interested
in women, was left a widower
without children, and you and I
are claimants for this country.
      You state in your behalf that you are
the daughter of his elder sister;
I claim that I am a male child
and thus, even though born to the younger sister,
I ought to be preferred over you.
      We reported to our uncle
your pretensions and mine;
he replied that he wished
to settle our dispute, and we agreed upon
this place and day for it.

Con esta intención salí
de Moscovia y de su tierra;
con ésta llegué hasta aquí,
en vez de haceros yo guerra,
a que me la hagáis a mí.
    ¡Oh! quiera Amor, sabio dios,
que el vulgo, astrólogo cierto,
hoy lo sea con los dos,
y que pare este concierto
en que seáis reina vos;
    pero reina en mi albedrío,
dándoos, para más honor,
su corona nuestro tío,
sus triunfos vuestro valor,
y su imperio el amor mío.

EST.:   A tan cortés bizarría,
menos mi pecho no muestra,
pues la imperial monarquía,
para sólo hacerla vuestra
me holgara que fuese mía;
    aunque no está satisfecho
mi amor de que sois ingrato,
si en cuanto decís sospecho
que os desmiente ese retrato
que está pendiente del pecho.

AST.:   Satisfaceros intento
con él; mas lugar no da
tanto sonoro instrumento,
que avisa que sale ya
el rey con su Parlamento.

Tocan, y sale el REY BASILIO, *viejo, y acompañamiento.*

EST.:   Sabio Tales,
AST.:   docto Euclides,
EST.:   que entre signos,
AST.:   .   que entre estrellas,
EST.:   hoy gobiernas,
AST.:   hoy resides,

        With this in mind I set out
from Muscovy and its lands;
with this in mind I arrived here,
instead of declaring war on you,
so that you could declare it on me.
        Oh, may Love, that wise god, grant
that the common people—such accurate astrologers!—
may be so today in regard to both of us,
and that this concord may result
in your becoming the queen—
        but the queen of my free choice,
with our uncle giving you
his crown, for greater honor,
your merit giving you its triumphs,
and my love giving you its dominion!

EST.:   In the face of such courtly generosity,
my heart displays an equal one,
since I'd be glad if the sovereign
monarchy were mine,
merely in order to pass it on to you;
        and yet, my love is poorly gratified
by your infidelity,
when I suspect, despite all you say,
that your words are belied by that portrait
hanging on your breast.

AST.:   I intend to placate your misgivings
in that regard; but the occasion is cut short
by all those ringing trumpets
which announce that the king
and his council are now entering.

Trumpets sound and the aged king BASILIO *enters with a retinue.*

EST.:   Wise Thales,[10]. . .
AST.:   Learned Euclid,
EST.:   you who amid the Zodiac . . .
AST.:   you who amid stars . . .
EST.:   are ruler today, . . .
AST.:   reside today, . . .

---

10. An Ancient Greek philosopher. In this passage, Estrella's half-lines form a continuous speech, as do Astolfo's.

EST.:   y sus caminos,

AST.:   sus huellas

EST.:   describes,

AST.:   tasas y mides . . .

EST.:   deja que en humildes lazos,

AST.:   deja que en tiernos abrazos

EST.:   hiedra de ese tronco sea,

AST.:   rendido a tus pies me vea.

BAS.:   Sobrinos, dadme los brazos,
         y creed, pues que, leales
       a mi precepto amoroso,
       venís con afectos tales,
       que a nadie deje quejoso
       y los dos quedéis iguales;
         y así cuando me confieso,
       rendido al prolijo peso,
       sólo os pido en la ocasión
       silencio, que admiración
       ha de pedirla el suceso.
         Ya sabéis, estadme atentos,
       amados sobrinos míos,
       corte ilustre de Polonia,
       vasallos, deudos y amigos;
       ya sabéis que yo en el mundo,
       por mi ciencia he merecido
       el sobrenombre de docto;
       pues, contra el tiempo y olvido,
       los pinceles de Timantes,
       los mármoles de Lisipo,
       en el ámbito del orbe
       me aclaman el gran Basilio.
       Ya sabéis que son las ciencias
       que más curso y más estimo,
       matemáticas sutiles,
       por quien al tiempo le quito,
       por quien a la fama rompo
       la jurisdicción y oficio
       de enseñar más cada día;

EST.:   you who describe . . .

AST.:   you who assess and measure

EST.:   the paths of their stars, . . .

AST.:   their traces in the sky, . . .

EST.:   permit me, in humble windings, . . .

AST.:   permit me, in tender embraces, . . .

EST.:   to be the ivy clinging to you, the tree!

AST.:   to see myself stretched at your feet!

BAS.:   Niece and nephew, embrace me,
       and be assured, since, faithful
to my loving command,
you have come here so affectionately,
that I shall leave neither of you lamenting
and that you will be treated with equity;
       and so, while I make a confession,
succumbing to an excessive burden,
I merely ask you on this occasion
for silence—because astonishment
will ensue from the very events!
       You already know—pay close heed to me!—
you, my beloved niece and nephew,
you the illustrious court of Poland,
vassals, kinsmen, and friends;
you already know that throughout the world
my scientific pursuits have won me
the appellation "learned";
for—in despite of Time and oblivion—
the brushes of Timanthes
and the marbles of Lysippus[11]
in the whole circle of the globe
acclaim me as the great Basilio.
You already know that the science
I chiefly study and esteem is
subtle mathematics,
by which I steal from Time
and ravish from Fame
their jurisdiction and their function
of teaching men more every day;

---

11. Two Greek artists of the 4th century B.C. Calderón wrote a play about the painter Timanthes. The sculptor Lysippus worked for Alexander the Great.

pues cuando en mis tablas miro
presentes las novedades
de los venideros siglos,
le gano al tiempo las gracias
de contar lo que yo he dicho.
Esos círculos de nieve,
esos doseles de vidrio,
que el sol ilumina a rayos,
que parte la luna a giros;
esos orbes de diamantes,
esos globos cristalinos,
que las estrellas adornan
y que campean los signos,
son el estudio mayor
de mis años, son los libros,
donde en papel de diamante,
en cuadernos de zafiros,
escribe con líneas de oro,
en caracteres distintos
el cielo nuestros sucesos
ya adversos o ya benignos.
Estos leo tan veloz,
que con mi espíritu sigo
sus rápidos movimientos
por rumbos y por caminos.
¡Pluguiera al cielo, primero
que mi ingenio hubiera sido
de sus márgenes comento
y de sus hojas registro,
hubiera sido mi vida
el primero desperdicio
de sus iras, y que en ellas
mi tragedia hubiera sido,
porque de los infelices
aun el mérito es cuchillo;
¡que a quien le daña el saber,
homicida es de sí mismo!
Dígalo yo, aunque mejor
lo dirán sucesos míos,
para cuya admiración
otra vez silencio os pido.

because, when I see present
in my charts the future events
of ages to come,
I win from Time men's gratitude
for recounting what I have said.
Those rings of snow,
those canopies of glass,
which the sun illuminates with its beams,
which the moon separates with its revolutions;
those globes of diamond,
those spheres of crystal,
which the stars adorn
and the constellations occupy,
are the principal study
of my years, they are the books
in which, on diamond paper,
on sapphire signatures,
heaven writes in golden lines
and distinct characters
the events of our lives,
sometimes adverse, sometimes beneficent.
I read these books so swiftly
that with my spirit I follow
their rapid movements
along their courses and paths.
Would that it had pleased heaven, before
my intelligence ever became
the marginal commentary to those books
and the index to their pages,
to make my life
the first victim
of its wrath, and to let that wrath
constitute my sole tragedy!—
because, for unlucky people,
even their merit is a sharp knife,
since the man harmed by his own knowledge
is a self-murderer!
Let me say this, even though the events of my life
will state it more plainly;
so that you may marvel at them,
once again I ask you to be silent.

En Clorilene mi esposa,
tuve un infelice hijo,
en cuyo parto los cielos
se agotaron de prodigios,
antes que a la luz hermosa
le diese el sepulcro vivo
de un vientre, porque el nacer
y el morir son parecidos.
Su madre infinitas veces,
entre ideas y delirios
del sueño, vio que rompía
sus entrañas atrevido
un monstruo en forma de hombre,
y entre su sangre teñido,
le daba muerte, naciendo
víbora humana del siglo.
Llegó de su parto el día
y, los presagios cumplidos
(porque tarde o nunca son
mentirosos los impíos),
nació en horóscopo tal,
que el sol, en su sangre tinto,
entraba sañudamente
con la luna en desafío;
y siendo valla la tierra,
los dos faroles divinos
a luz entera luchaban,
ya que no a brazo partido.
El mayor, el más horrendo
eclipse que ha padecido
el sol, después que con sangre
lloró la muerte de Cristo,
éste fue; porque anegado
el orbe entre incendios vivos,
presumió que padecía
el último parasismo.
Los cielos se oscurecieron,
temblaron los edificios,
llovieron piedras las nubes,
corrieron sangre los ríos.

By Clorilene my wife
I had an unlucky son,
during whose gestation the heavens
exhausted their miracles
even before he emerged into the lovely light
from the living grave
of the womb (because birth
and death are similar).
Infinite times his mother,
amid the visions and delirium
of dreams, saw her entrails
being burst by a bold
monster in human shape;
dyed in her blood,
he was killing her, born
to be the human viper of the age.
The day of her delivery arrived
and, the forecasts coming true
(because evil forecasts never lie,
or, if so, only belatedly),
he was born at such an astrological conjunction
that the sun, tinged with its blood,
was fiercely entering
into a joust with the moon,
and, with the earth for their barrier,
the two celestial lamps
were struggling light to light,
since one cannot say "hand to hand."
The greatest, most terrifying
eclipse ever suffered by
the sun from the time when it bloodily
bewailed the death of Christ,
was this one: because the globe,
drowned in living flames,
seemed to be suffering
its final paroxysm.
The sky was darkened,
buildings shook,
the clouds rained stones,
the rivers ran blood.

En este mísero, en este
mortal planeta o signo
nació Segismundo, dando
de su condición indicios,
pues dio la muerte a su madre,
con cuya fiereza dijo:
hombre soy, pues que ya empiezo
a pagar mal beneficios.
Yo, acudiendo a mis estudios,
en ellos y en todo miro
que Segismundo sería
el hombre más atrevido,
el príncipe más cruel
y el monarca más impío,
por quien su reino vendría
a ser parcial y diviso,
escuela de las traiciones
y academia de los vicios;
y él, de su furor llevado,
entre asombros y delitos,
había de poner en mí
las plantas, y yo rendido
a sus pies me había de ver:
(¡con qué congoja lo digo!)
siendo alfombra de sus plantas
las canas del rostro mío.
¿Quién no da crédito al daño,
y más al daño que ha visto
en su estudio, donde hace
el amor propio su oficio?
Pues dando crédito yo
a los hados, que, adivinos,
me pronosticaban daños
en fatales vaticinios,
determiné de encerrar
la fiera que había nacido,
por ver si el sabio tenía
en las estrellas dominio.
Publicóse que el infante
nació muerto y, prevenido,
hice labrar una torre

Under this unhappy, under this
fatal planet or sign
Segismundo was born, giving
an indication of his nature,
because he killed his mother.
By this cruelty he was saying:
"I am a man, since I am already beginning
to repay kindness with evil."
I, referring to my books,
found in them, and in all things,
that Segismundo would be
the most insolent man,
the most cruel prince,
and the most impious monarch,
through whom his kingdom would come
to be fragmented and divided,
a school for treason
and an academy of vice;
and that he, carried away by his fury,
amid fearful crimes,
would one day set his foot
on me, and that I, surrendering,
would find myself groveling before him
(with what anguish I say this!),
the gray hairs of my beard
serving as a carpet to his feet.
Who doesn't believe in coming harm,
especially in harm that has been revealed
to him by his own studies, in which case
self-love plays an additional part?
Well, I, lending credence
to soothsaying fate,
which forecast harm to me
in dire predictions,
decided to lock up
the wild beast that had been born,
to see whether a wise man
can prevail over the stars.
It was announced that the prince
was stillborn and, as a precaution,
I had a tower erected

entre las peñas y riscos
de esos montes, donde apenas
la luz ha hallado camino,
por defenderle la entrada
sus rústicos obeliscos.
Las graves penas y leyes,
que con públicos edictos
declararon que ninguno
entrase a un vedado ·sitio
del monte, se ocasionaron
de las causas que os he dicho.
Allí Segismundo vive,
mísero, pobre y cautivo,
adonde sólo Clotaldo
le ha hablado, tratado y visto:
éste le ha enseñado ciencias,
éste en la ley le ha instruido
católica, siendo solo
de sus miserias testigo.
Aquí hay tres cosas: la una,
que yo, Polonia, os estimo
tanto, que os quiero librar
de la opresión y servicio
de un rey tirano, porque
no fuera señor benigno
el que a su patria y su imperio
pusiera en tanto peligro.
La otra es considerar
que si a mi sangre le quito
el derecho que le dieron
humano fuero y divino,
no es cristiana caridad,
pues ninguna ley ha dicho
que por reservar yo a otro
de tirano y de atrevido,
pueda yo serlo, supuesto
que si es tirano mi hijo,
porque él delitos no haga,
vengo yo a hacer los delitos.
Es la última y tercera,
el ver cuánto yerro ha sido

amid the rocks and crags
of those mountains, where light
has scarcely found a way in,
because their rugged obelisks
bar its entry.
The severe penalties of the law,
which in public edicts
ordered that no one
should enter a forbidden place
in the mountains, were occasioned
by the reasons I have stated.
There Segismundo lives,
wretched, poor, a captive,
where only Clotaldo
has spoken to him, kept him company, and seen him;
Clotaldo has taught him sciences,
and has instructed him in the Catholic
religion, being the only
witness to his misery.
Now, in all this there are three factors at play: one,
people of Poland, is that I love you
so much that I wish to free you
from oppressive service
to a tyrannical king, because
one who would place his homeland
and his realm in such peril
wouldn't be a kindly king.
The second factor is the reflection
that my depriving my own flesh and blood
of the rights he was given
by both human and divine law
is not Christian charity,
because no law ever stated
that, to prevent another man
from being tyrannical and insolent,
I should act that way myself—since,
even if my son is a potential tyrant,
to stop him from committing crimes,
I myself come to commit them.
The third and final factor
is the realization that it was a tremendous mistake

dar crédito fácilmente
a los sucesos previstos;
pues aunque su inclinación
le dicte sus precipicios,
quizá no le vencerán,
porque el hado más esquivo,
la inclinación más violenta,
el planeta más impío,
sólo el albedrío inclinan,
no fuerzan el albedrío.
Y así, entre una y otra causa,
vacilante y discursivo,
previne un remedio tal
que os suspenda los sentidos.
Yo he de ponerle mañana,
sin que él sepa que es mi hijo
y rey vuestro, a Segismundo
(que aqueste su nombre ha sido)
en mi dosel, en mi silla,
y, en fin, en el lugar mío,
donde os gobierne y os mande
y donde todos rendidos
la obediencia le juréis;
pues con aquesto consigo
tres cosas, con que respondo
a las otras tres que he dicho.
Es la primera, que siendo
prudente, cuerdo y benigno,
desmintiendo en todo al hado
que de él tantas cosas dijo,
gozaréis el natural
príncipe vuestro, que ha sido
cortesano de unos montes
y de sus fieras vecino.
Es la segunda, que si él,
soberbio, osado, atrevido
y cruel, con rienda suelta
corre el campo de sus vicios,
habré yo piadoso entonces
con mi obligación cumplido,
y luego en desposeerle

to lend easy credence
to the predictions of events;
because, even if his nature
is inclined toward outrages,
perhaps it won't overcome him,
since even the most dire fate,
the most violent inclination,
the most evil planet,
merely dispose our free will in a certain direction,
but never compel it in that direction.
And so, what with one reason and another,
in my vacillating meditations
I hit upon a solution of such a kind
that it will numb your senses.
Tomorrow, without his knowing
that he is my son and your king,
I shall place Segismundo
(for that is his name)
on my throne, beneath my canopy—
in short, in my place—
where he will govern and rule you
and where all of you submissively
will swear obedience to him;
because, by doing this, I achieve
three things, with which I respond
to the three other factors that I mentioned.
First: if he is
prudent, sane, and beneficent,
and completely gives the lie to the prophecy
that said all those things about him,
you will enjoy the presence of your
natural prince, who has been
the courtier of mountains
and neighbor to their wild animals.
Second: if he
haughtily, boldly, insolently,
and cruelly gives free rein
to his vices and they run away with him,
in that case I shall have mercifully
complied with my obligations,
and by dispossessing him at that time

haré como rey invicto,
siendo el volverle a la cárcel
no crueldad, sino castigo.
Es la tercera, que siendo
el príncipe como os digo,
por lo que os amo, vasallos,
os daré reyes más dignos
de la corona y el cetro;
pues serán mis dos sobrinos,
que junto en uno el derecho
de los dos, y convenidos
con la fe del matrimonio,
tendrán lo que han merecido.
Esto como rey os mando,
esto como padre os pido,
esto como sabio os ruego,
esto como anciano os digo.
Y si el Séneca español,
que era humilde esclavo, dijo,
de su república un rey,
como esclavo os lo suplico.

AST.:   Si a mí el responder me toca
como el que en efecto ha sido
aquí el más interesado,
en nombre de todos digo
que Segismundo parezca,
pues le basta ser tu hijo.

TODOS: Danos al príncipe nuestro
que ya por rey le pedimos.

BAS.:   Vasallos, esa fineza
os agradezco y estimo.
Acompañad a sus cuartos
a los dos Atlantes míos,
que mañana le veréis.

TODOS: ¡Viva el grande rey Basilio!

Entranse todos. Antes que se entre el REY,
sale CLOTALDO, ROSAURA *y* CLARÍN, *y detiene al* REY.

CLO.:   ¿Podréte hablar?

I shall be acting like an unconquered king,
since returning him to his prison
will be not cruelty, but a punishment.
Third: if the prince
is really as I have just stated,
out of my love for you, my vassals,
I shall give you monarchs more worthy
of the crown and scepter;
for they will be my niece and nephew,
because I join together their separate
claims, and, brought into agreement
by the sacrament of marriage,
they will both have what they have deserved.
This I command you as king,
this I ask of you as a father,
this I request of you as a philosopher,
this I state to you as an elderly man.
And, if Seneca[12] of Spain once said
that a king is the humble slave
of his commonwealth,
this I beseech of you as a slave.

AST.:   If it is my due to reply,
since I have indeed been
the man with most at stake here,
in the name of all I say:
let Segismundo appear,
because it is enough that he is your son.

ALL: Give us our prince,
whom we already request as our king!

BAS.:   Vassals, for these kind words
I thank and esteem you.
Escort to their rooms
these two props of my old age,
for tomorrow you shall see him.

ALL: Long live the great king Basilio!

All exit. Before BASILIO *completes his exit,* CLOTALDO, ROSAURA,
and CLARÍN *enter, and* CLOTALDO *detains* BASILIO.

CLO.:   May I speak with you?

---

12. The Roman philosopher of the 1st century A.D., born in Spain.

Bas.:   ¡Oh, Clotaldo!
         Tú seas muy bien venido.
Clo.:   Aunque viniendo a tus plantas
         es fuerza el haberlo sido,
         esta vez rompe, señor,
         el hado triste y esquivo
         el privilegio a la ley
         y a la costumbre el estilo.
Bas.:   ¿Qué tienes?
Clo.:   Una desdicha,
         señor, que me ha sucedido,
         cuando pudiera tenerla
         por el mayor regocijo.
Bas.:   Prosigue.
Clo.:   Este bello joven,
         osado o inadvertido,
         entró en la torre, señor,
         adonde al príncipe ha visto.
         Y es . . .
Bas.:   No te aflijas, Clotaldo.
         Si otro día hubiera sido,
         confieso que lo sintiera;
         pero ya el secreto he dicho,
         y no importa que él lo sepa,
         supuesto que yo lo digo.
         Vedme después, porque tengo
         muchas cosas que advertiros,
         y muchas que hagáis por mí;
         que habéis de ser, os aviso,
         instrumento del mayor
         suceso que el mundo ha visto.
         Y a esos presos, porque al fin
         no presumáis que castigo
         descuidos vuestros, perdono.   (*Vase.*)
Clo.:   ¡Vivas, gran señor, mil siglos!
         Mejoró el cielo la suerte.
         Ya no diré que es mi hijo,
         pues que lo puedo excusar.
         Extranjeros peregrinos,
         libres estáis.
Ros.:   Tus pies beso

BAS.:   Oh, Clotaldo!
A hearty welcome to you!

CLO.:   Even though my arrival in your presence
necessarily implies that I have "come well,"
this time, Sire, a sad
and malignant fate violates
the privilege of the law
and the good manners of custom.

BAS.:   What's wrong with you?

CLO.:   Sire, it's
a misfortune that has befallen me
just when I had the right to consider the event
as the greatest cause for rejoicing.

BAS.:   Go on.

CLO.:   This handsome youth,
whether through boldness or carelessness,
entered the tower, Sire,
where he caught sight of the prince.
And he's . . .

BAS.:   Don't fret, Clotaldo.
If it had occurred on any other day,
I confess that I would have been sorry for it;
but now I have divulged the secret,
and it doesn't matter that he knows it,
seeing that I have told it.
See me later, because I have
many things to inform you about,
and many for you to do for me;
because, let me tell you, you are to be
the agent of the greatest
event in the history of the world.
As for these captives, in order that you don't end up
imagining that I am punishing them
for your carelessness, I pardon them.   (*Exit.*)

CLO.:   Great lord, may you live a thousand centuries!
(*Aside:*) Heaven has improved my lot.
Now I won't report that he's my son,
seeing that I can exonerate him.
(*Aloud:*) Wandering strangers,
you are at liberty.

ROS.:   I venerate your feet

mil veces.

CLA.:   Y yo los viso;
que una letra más o menos
no reparan dos amigos.

ROS.:   La vida, señor, me has dado,
y pues a tu cuenta vivo,
eternamente seré
esclavo tuyo.

CLO.:   No ha sido
vida la que yo te ha dado,
porque un hombre bien nacido,
si está agraviado no vive;
y supuesto que has venido
a vengarte de un agravio,
según tú propio me has dicho,
no te he dado vida yo,
porque tú no la has traído;
que vida infame no es vida.
(Bien con aquesto le animo.)   (*Aparte.*)

ROS.:   Confieso que no la tengo
aunque de ti la recibo;
pero yo con la venganza
dejaré mi honor tan limpio
que pueda mi vida luego,
atropellando peligros,
parecer dádiva tuya.

CLO.:   Toma el acero bruñido
que trujiste, que yo sé
que él baste, en sangre teñido
de tu enemigo, a vengarte;
porque acero que fue mío
(digo este instante, este rato
que en mi poder le he tenido),
sabrá vengarte.

ROS.:   En tu nombre
segunda vez me le ciño,
y en él juro mi venganza,

with a thousand kisses.

CLA.: And I validate them;
because, between friends, a few letters in a word
make no difference.[13]

ROS.: My lord, you have given me my life,
and since I am alive on your account,
I shall eternally be
your slave.

CLO.: It wasn't
life that I gave you,
because when a man of good birth
has been affronted, he's not alive;
and since you have come
to take revenge for an affront,
as you yourself have told me,
I haven't given you life,
because you didn't come here with it;
for a vile life is no life at all.
(*Aside:*) With these words I'll stir him to action.

ROS.: I confess that I don't have life
even though I receive it from you;
but, with my revenge, I
shall leave my honor so clean
that, afterwards, my life,
trampling all dangers,
will seem to be a gift from you.

CLO.: Take back this burnished steel
that you were wearing, for I know
it is sufficient, when dyed in the blood
of your enemy, to avenge you;
because steel that once was mine
(I mean just this moment, this while
that I have had it in my keeping)
will be able to avenge you.

ROS.: In your name
I gird it on for the second time,
and on it I swear my revenge,

---

13. In the Spanish original, the pun is less cumbersome, though equally gratuitous. Clarín echoes Rosaura's *beso* ("I kiss") with *viso* ("I give my official stamp of approval"). He speaks of only one letter's difference (*i* for *e*) because the *b* and the *v* have the same sound. Other editors read *piso* ("I step on [them]").

aunque fuese mi enemigo
más poderoso.

CLO.:   ¿Eslo mucho?

ROS.:   Tanto, que no te lo digo,
no porque de tu prudencia
mayores cosas no fío,
sino porque no se vuelva
contra mí el favor que admiro
en tu piedad.

CLO.:   Antes fuera
ganarme a mí con decirlo;
pues fuera cerrarme el paso
de ayudar a tu enemigo.
¡Oh, si supiera quién es!   (*Aparte.*)

ROS.:   Porque no pienses que estimo
tan poco esa confianza,
sabe que el contrario ha sido
no menos que Astolfo, duque
de Moscovia.

CLO.:   Mal resisto   (*Aparte*)
el dolor, porque es más grave
que fue imaginado, visto.
Apuremos más el caso.
Si moscovita has nacido,
el que es natural señor
mal agraviarte ha podido;
vuélvete a tu patria, pues,
y deja el ardiente brío
que te despeña.

ROS.:   Yo sé
que, aunque mi príncipe ha sido,
pudo agraviarme.

CLO.:   No pudo,
aunque pusiera atrevido
la mano en tu rostro. (¡Ay cielos!)

ROS.:   Mayor fue el agravio mío.

CLO.:   Dilo ya, pues que no puedes
decir más que yo imagino.

ROS.:   Si dijera; mas no sé
con qué respeto te miro,
con qué afecto te venero,

no matter how powerful my enemy
may be.
CLO.:   Is he very much so?
ROS.:   So much so, that I won't tell you his name;
not because I wouldn't trust
your prudence with even greater things,
but in order that your partiality toward me,
which I wonder at in seeing your kindness,
won't turn against me.
CLO.:   On the contrary, you'd be
winning me over by telling me;
because it would mean preventing me
from aiding your enemy.
(*Aside:*) Oh, if I only knew who he was!
ROS.:   So that you won't think I hold
your confidence so cheaply,
let me tell you that my opponent is
none other than Astolfo, Duke
of Muscovy.
CLO.:   (*Aside:*) I can't abide
this grief, because, known, it is
greater than when I just imagined it.
Let us look into the matter further.
(*Aloud:*) If you are a Muscovite born,
the man who is your natural lord
can't really have affronted you;
so, return to your homeland
and abandon this ardent desire
which will destroy you.
ROS.:   I know
that, even though he was my prince,
he did actually affront me.
CLO.:   He couldn't have,
even if he insolently slapped
your face. (Oh, heavens!)
ROS.:   The affront to me was greater yet.
CLO.:   Then tell me what it was, because you can't
say more than I imagine.
ROS.:   I would tell you, but I don't know
what respect for you as I behold you,
what affection for you as I venerate you,

con qué estimación te asisto,
que no me atrevo a decirte
que es este exterior vestido
enigma, pues no es de quien
parece: juzga advertido,
si no soy lo que parezco,
y Astolfo a casarse vino
con Estrella, si podrá
agraviarme. Harto te he dicho.

Vanse ROSAURA *y* CLARÍN.

CLO.:   ¡Escucha, aguarda, detente!
¿Qué confuso laberinto
es éste, donde no puede
hallar la razón el hilo?
Mi honor es el agraviado,
poderoso el enemigo,
yo vasallo, ella mujer,
descubra el cielo camino;
aunque no sé si podrá
cuando en tan confuso abismo,
es todo el cielo un presagio
y es todo el mundo un prodigio.

what esteem for you as I attend you,
makes me lack the courage to tell you
that these external trappings of mine
are a riddle, because the one they clothe
isn't what he seems. With this hint, judge—
if I'm not what I seem,
and if Astolfo has come here to marry
Estrella—whether he is capable
of affronting me. I've told you enough.

ROSAURA *and* CLARÍN *exit.*

CLO.:   Listen! Wait! Stop!
What muddled labyrinth
is this, in which reason
cannot find the guiding thread?
It is my own honor that has been affronted,
the enemy is powerful,
I am a vassal, she is a woman—
let heaven discover the right path!
Though I don't know if that's possible
when, in such a confusing abyss,
all of heaven is one great omen
and the whole world one great marvel!

Jornada segunda

Salen el REY BASILIO *y* CLOTALDO.

CLO.:   Todo como lo mandaste,
         queda efectuado.
BAS.:   Cuenta,
         Clotaldo, cómo pasó.
CLO.:   Fue, señor, desta manera.
         Con la apacible bebida,
         que de confecciones llena
         hacer mandaste, mezclando
         la virtud de algunas yerbas
         cuyo tirano poder
         y cuya secreta fuerza
         así el humano discurso
         priva, roba y enajena,
         que deja vivo cadáver
         a un hombre, y cuya violencia,
         adormecido, le quita
         los sentidos y potencias . . .
         No tenemos que argüir,
         que aquesto posible sea,
         pues tantas veces, señor,
         nos ha dicho la experiencia,
         y es cierto, que de secretos
         naturales está llena
         la medicina, y no hay
         animal, planta ni piedra
         que no tenga calidad
         determinada; y si llega
         a examinar mil venenos
         la humana malicia nuestra,

58

Act Two

Enter BASILIO *and* CLOTALDO.

CLO.: Everything you ordered
has been carried out.

BAS.:   Tell me
how things went, Clotaldo.

CLO.: It was this way, Sire.
With the soporific potion,
filled with various compounds,
that you ordered to be brewed, mingling into it
the power of certain herbs
whose tyrannical force
and secret strength
deprives, robs, and dispossesses
a man of his reasoning powers so drastically
that he remains a living corpse,
and whose violence
puts him to sleep and takes away
his senses and abilities . . .
There's no need for us to debate
whether such things are possible,
because experience, Sire,
has informed us of it so often,
and it's verified that the medical art
is full of natural
mysteries, and that there's no
animal, plant, or stone
that doesn't possess given
powers; and if our
human cunning is able
to concoct a thousand poisons

59

que den la muerte, ¿qué mucho
que, templada su violencia,
pues hay venenos que maten,
haya venenos que aduerman?
Dejando aparte el dudar,
si es posible que suceda,
pues que ya queda probado
con razones y evidencias;
con la bebida, en efecto,
que el opio, la adormidera
y el beleño compusieron,
bajé a la cárcel estrecha
de Segismundo; con él
hablé un rato de las letras
humanas que le ha enseñado
la muda naturaleza
de los montes y los cielos,
en cuya divina escuela
la retórica aprendió
de las aves y las fieras.
Para levantarle más
el espíritu a la empresa
que solicitas, tomé
por asunto la presteza
de un águila caudalosa,
que despreciando la esfera
del viento, pasaba a ser,
en las regiones supremas
del fuego, rayo de pluma
o desasido cometa.
Encarecí el vuelo altivo,
diciendo: "Al fin eres reina
de las aves, y así, a todas
es justo que te prefieras."
El no hubo menester más;
que en tocando esta materia
de la majestad, discurre
con ambición y soberbia;
porque, en efecto, la sangre
le incita, mueve y alienta
a cosas grandes, y dijo:

capable of killing, what wonder is it
if, once their violence is mitigated,
since there are poisons that can kill,
there should be poisons that put a man to sleep?
Setting aside doubts
as to the possibility of such an occurrence,
since it has already been proved
by reasoning and evidence—
to return to the case before us, with the potion
compounded of opium, poppy,
and henbane
I descended to Segismundo's
cramped dungeon; I spoke
with him for a while about
the humanities in which he has been instructed
by the wordless nature
of mountains and skies,
in whose divine school
he has learned the rhetoric
of birds and beasts.
In order to raise his spirit
higher, with a view to the undertaking
you have in mind for him, I took
as my subject the swiftness
of a mighty eagle,
which, scorning the sphere
of the wind, was ascending in order to become,
in the supreme regions
of fire, a feathered thunderbolt
or a comet detached from its orbit.
I praised its bold flight,
saying: "In short, you are queen
of the birds, and so it is only right
for you to lord it over them all."
He needed no further prompting;
because, upon this topic
of kingship, he discourses
with ambition and pride;
since, in reality, his blood
prompts him, stirs him, and incites him
to lofty actions; and he said:

"¿Que en la república inquieta
de las aves también haya
quien les jure la obediencia?
En llegando a este discurso,
mis desdichas me consuelan;
pues por lo menos si estoy
sujeto, lo estoy por fuerza;
porque voluntariamente
a otro hombre no me rindiera."
Viéndole ya enfurecido
con esto, que ha sido el tema
de su dolor, le brindé
con la pócima, y apenas
pasó desde el vaso al pecho
el licor, cuando las fuerzas
rindió al sueño, discurriendo
por los miembros y las venas
un sudor frío, de modo,
que a no saber yo que era
muerte fingida, dudara
de su vida. En esto llegan
las gentes de quien tú fías
el valor de esta experiencia,
y poniéndole en un coche
hasta tu cuarto le llevan
donde prevenida estaba
la majestad y grandeza
que es digna de su persona.
Allí en tu cama le acuestan,
donde al tiempo que el letargo
haya perdido la fuerza,
como a ti mismo, señor,
le sirvan, que así lo ordenas.
Y si haberte obedecido
te obliga a que yo merezca
galardón, sólo te pido
(perdona mi inadvertencia)
que me digas ¿qué es tu intento
trayendo de esta manera
a Segismundo a palacio?
BAS.:   Clotaldo, muy justa es esa

"So, then, even in the restless commonwealth
of the birds there are some
who swear obedience to others?
When I arrive at this reasoning,
my misfortunes console me;
since, at least, if I am
a subject, I am one under compulsion;
because I wouldn't submit
to another man of my own free will."
Seeing him now roused to fury
by this, which has been the subject
of his sorrow, I offered him
the beverage, and no sooner
did the liquid pass from the tumbler
to his bosom than he yielded up
his strength to slumber, a cold sweat
running through his limbs
and veins, so that,
had I not known it was
merely a semblance of death, I would have feared
for his life. At that moment there arrived
the people to whom you are entrusting
the value of this experiment,
and, placing him in a carriage,
they bore him to your apartment,
where there stood in readiness
the royal grandeur
worthy of his person.
There they put him in your bed,
where, whenever the lethargy
has lost its strength,
they will serve him, Sire,
as they would you, for such are your orders.
And, if my obedience to you
obliges you to consider me deserving
of a reward, I merely ask you
(pardon my indiscretion)
to tell me what you have in mind
by bringing Segismundo
to the palace this way.

BAS.: Clotaldo, this uncertainty of yours

duda que tienes, y quiero
sólo a vos satisfacerla.
A Segismundo, mi hijo,
el influjo de su estrella
(bien lo sabéis) amenaza
mil desdichas y tragedias;
quiero examinar si el cielo,
(que no es posible que mienta,
y más habiéndonos dado
de su rigor tantas muestras
en su cruel condición),
o se mitiga, o se templa
por lo menos, y vencido
con valor y con prudencia,
se desdice; porque el hombre
predomina en las estrellas.
Esto quiero examinar,
trayéndole donde sepa
que es mi hijo, y donde haga
de su talento la prueba.
Si magnánimo se vence,
reinará; pero si muestra
el ser cruel y tirano,
le volveré a su cadena.
Ahora preguntarás,
que para aquesta experiencia
¿qué importó haberle traído
dormido desta manera?
Y quiero satisfacerte
dándote a todo respuesta.
Si él supiera que es mi hijo
hoy, y mañana se viera
segunda vez reducido
a su prisión y miseria,
cierto es de su condición
que desesperara en ella;
porque sabiendo quién es,
¿qué consuelo habrá que tenga?
Y así he querido dejar
abierta al daño esta puerta
del decir que fue soñado

is quite justified, and I wish
to resolve it for you alone.
Segismundo, my son,
as you well know, is threatened
by the influence of his natal planet
with a thousand misfortunes and tragedies;
I wish to determine whether heaven
(which cannot lie,
especially after giving us
such great displays of its severity
with regard to his cruel nature)
can be assuaged, or at least
mollified, and whether, overcome
by merit and wisdom,
it can go back on its word; because man
has dominion over the stars.
This I wish to determine
by bringing him to a place where he will learn
that he is my son, and where I can
put his character to the test.
If, by his highmindedness, he conquers his nature,
he shall reign; but if he displays
a cruel and tyrannical nature,
I shall send him back to his chains.
Now you will ask
why, for this experiment,
it was necessary to bring him here
asleep like this.
And I wish to content you
by giving you a full answer.
If he learned today that he is
my son, and found himself tomorrow
once again confined
in his wretched prison,
his character ensures us
that he would be in despair there;
because, if he knew who he is,
what consolation could he possibly have?
And so, I wanted to leave
a way out of that damaging situation:
to say that all he saw

cuanto vio. Con esto llegan
a examinarse dos cosas:
su condición la primera,
pues él despierto procede
en cuanto imagina y piensa;
y el consuelo la segunda,
pues aunque ahora se vea
obedecido, y después
a sus prisiones se vuelva,
podrá entender que soñó,
y hará bien cuando lo entienda,
porque en el mundo, Clotaldo,
todos los que viven sueñan.

CLO.: Razones no me faltaran
para probar que no aciertas,
mas ya no tiene remedio,
y según dicen las señas,
parece que ha despertado
y hacia nosotros se acerca.

BAS.: Yo me quiero retirar;
tú, como ayo suyo, llega,
y de tantas confusiones
como su discurso cercan,
le saca con la verdad.

CLO.: En fin, ¿que me das licencia
para que lo diga?

BAS.:   Sí;
que podrá ser, con saberla,
que, conocido el peligro,
más fácilmente se venza.

Vase y sale CLARÍN.

CLA.: A costa de cuatro palos,
que el llegar aquí me cuesta,
de un alabardero rubio
que barbó de su librea,
tengo de ver cuanto pasa;
que no hay ventana más cierta

was in a dream. This way, two things
can be tested:
first of all, his character,
because, when awake, he will behave
in accordance with his imaginings and thoughts;
secondly, the matter of his consolation,
since, even though he now finds himself
obeyed, and later
will return to captivity,
he will be able to surmise that it was a dream;
and it will be a good thing for him to realize,
because in this world, Clotaldo,
everyone who lives is a dreamer.

CLO.: I'd have no lack of arguments
to prove that your ideas are wrong,
but by now it can't be helped,
and, to judge by all indications,
it seems that he has awakened
and is heading our way.

BAS.: I wish to withdraw;
you, as his tutor, go to him
and, by telling the truth, release him
from all the confusion
that will besiege his judgment.

CLO.: In short, you give me permission
to tell him?

BAS.: Yes,
because maybe, when he knows the truth,
he'll recognize the danger he's in
and will conquer himself more readily.

Exit BASILIO. *Enter* CLARÍN.

CLA.: At the cost of a few blows
that my coming here cost me,
dealt by an auburn-haired halberdier[14]
whose beard sprouted out of his livery, matching it in color,
I shall observe all that goes on;
because there's no window view of a street celebration[15]

---

14. This has been thought to refer to the royal guards in Spain, who, since the days of Emperor Charles V, had been recruited from Flanders or Germany.   15. Or even of a play performance at a *corral*.

que aquella que, sin rogar
a un ministro de boletas,
un hombre se trae consigo;
pues para todas las fiestas,
despojado y despejado,
se asoma a su desvergüenza.

CLO.: Este es Clarín, el criado
de aquélla (¡ay cielos!), de aquella
que, tratante de desdichas,
pasó a Polonia mi afrenta.
Clarín, ¿qué hay de nuevo?

CLA.:   Hay,
señor, que tu gran clemencia,
dispuesta a vengar agravios
de Rosaura, la aconseja
que tome su propio traje.

CLO.: Y es bien, porque no parezca
liviandad.

CLA.:   Hay que, mudando
su nombre, y tomando cuerda
nombre de sobrina tuya,
hoy tanto honor se acrecienta,
que dama en palacio ya
de la singular Estrella
vive.

CLO.:   Es bien que de una vez
tome su honor por mi cuenta.

CLA.: Hay que ella se está esperando
que ocasión y tiempo venga
en que vuelvas por su honor.

CLO.: Prevención segura es ésa;
que al fin el tiempo ha de ser
quien haga esas diligencias.

CLA.: Hay que ella está regalada,
servida como una reina,
en fe de sobrina tuya,
y hay que, viniendo con ella,
estoy yo muriendo de hambre
y nadie de mí se acuerda,
sin mirar que soy Clarín,
y que si el tal Clarín suena,

that you can be so sure of finding as the one that, without
asking a ticket dispenser for it,
a man carries along with himself,
because at every festival,
even if penniless and wiped out,
his own nerviness provides him with the place at the window.

CLO.: This is Clarín, the servant
of that woman (ah, heavens!), of the woman
who, dealing in bad luck,
has imported an affront against me into Poland.
Clarín, what's new?

CLA.:   The news is,
my lord, that your great clemency,
prepared to avenge Rosaura's
affronts, has advised her
to wear appropriate clothing.

CLO.: And rightly so, to avoid any appearance
of wantonness.

CLA.:   The news is also that, changing
her name, and shrewdly calling
herself your niece,
she has had so much honor heaped on her today
that she is now residing in the palace
as a lady-in-waiting to the illustrious
Estrella.

CLO.:   It's only right that, once and for all,
she should receive honor on my account.

CLA.: Further news: she's waiting
for the proper time and opportunity to come
when you'll take action in behalf of her honor.

CLO.: I call that a reliable expectation;
because eventually time itself
will take those measures.

CLA.: More news: she is being entertained
and served like a queen,
on the strength of being your niece;
and furthermore, though I arrived along with her,
I'm starving to death
and no one's paying attention to me,
despite the fact that my name means Clarion,
and that, if such a clarion blows,

podrá decir cuanto pasa
al rey, a Astolfo y a Estrella;
porque Clarín y criado
son dos cosas que se llevan
con el secreto muy mal;
y podrá ser, si me deja
el silencio de su mano,
se cante por mí esta letra:
Clarín que rompe el albor,
no suena mejor.

CLO.: Tu queja está bien fundada;
yo satisfaré tu queja.
y en tanto sírveme a mí.

CLA.: Pues ya Segismundo llega.

Salen MÚSICOS *cantando, y* CRIADOS *dando de vestir a* SEGISMUNDO,
que sale como asombrado.

SEG.: ¡Válgame el cielo! ¿qué veo?
¡Válgame el cielo! ¿qué miro?
Con poco espanto lo admiro,
con mucha duda lo creo.
    ¿Yo en palacios suntuosos?
¿Yo entre telas y brocados?
¿Yo cercado de criados
tan lucidos y briosos?
    ¿Yo despertar de dormir
en lecho tan excelente?
¿Yo en medio de tanta gente
que me sirva de vestir?
    Decir que sueño es engaño,
bien sé que despierto estoy.
¿Yo Segismundo no soy?
Dadme, cielos, desengaño.
    Decidme qué pudo ser
esto que a mi fantasía
sucedió mientras dormía,
que aquí me he llegado a ver.
    Pero sea lo que fuere,
¿quién me mete en discurrir?
Dejarme quiero servir,
y venga lo que viniere.

it might tell all that's going on
to the King, Astolfo, and Estrella;
because a clarion and a servant
are two things that are extremely
mismatched with secrecy;
and perhaps, if silence
lets me slip out of its grasp,
the following song may be sung with me in mind:
"A dawn-shattering clarion
isn't as loud as that."

CLO.: Your complaint is well founded;
I'll placate your complaint,
and, in the meantime, be my servant.

CLA.: But here comes Segismundo.

Enter MUSICIANS *singing, and* SERVANTS *dressing* SEGISMUNDO,
who enters as if dumbfounded.

SEG.: Heaven help me! What's this I see?
Heaven help me! What do I behold?
I marvel at it with little fear,
but I believe it only with great doubt.
    I in a luxurious palace?
I amid fabrics and brocade?
I surrounded by such well-dressed,
energetic servants?
    I awakening from sleep
in such an excellent bed?
I in the midst of so many people
helping me to dress?
    To say I'm dreaming is mistaken,
I know very well I'm awake.
Am I not Segismundo?
Heavens, clarify my confusion!
    Tell me what can have
happened to my mind
while I was asleep,
that makes me find myself here.
    But, whatever it may be,
who's forcing me to ponder it?
I want to let myself be served,
come what may.

CRI. 2.°:   ¡Qué melancólico está!
CRI. 1.°:   ¿Pues a quién le sucediera
esto, que no lo estuviera?
CLA.:   A mí.
CRI. 2.°:   Llega a hablarle ya.
CRI. 1.°:   ¿Volverán a cantar?
SEG.:   No,
no quiero que canten más.
CRI. 2.°:   Como tan suspenso estás,
quise divertirte.
SEG.:   Yo
no tengo de divertir
con sus voces mis pesares;
las músicas militares
sólo he gustado de oír.
CLO.:   Vuestra Alteza, gran señor,
me dé su mano a besar,
que el primero le ha de dar
esta obediencia mi honor.
SEG.:   Clotaldo es: ¿pues cómo así,
quien en prisión me maltrata,
con tal respeto me trata?
¿Qué es lo que pasa por mí?
CLO.:   Con la grande confusión
que el nuevo estado te da,
mil dudas padecerá
el discurso y la razón;
pero ya librarte quiero
de todas (si puede ser)
porque has, señor, de saber
que eres príncipe heredero
de Polonia. Si has estado
retirado y escondido,
por obedecer ha sido
a la inclemencia del hado,
que mil tragedias consiente
a este imperio, cuando en él
el soberano laurel
corone tu augusta frente.
Mas fiando a tu atención
que vencerás las estrellas,

SER. 2:   How melancholy he is!
SER. 1:   Well, who wouldn't be
          if this happened to him?
CLA.:   Me.
SER. 2:   Go over and talk to him now.
SER. 1:   Should they sing another song?
SEG.:   No,
          I don't want them to sing anymore.
SER. 2:   Since you're so distraught,
          I wanted to entertain you.
SEG.:   I
            don't need to divert
          my sorrows with their voices;
          martial music
          is the only kind I've enjoyed hearing.
CLO.:   Your Highness, great lord,
          give me your hand to kiss,
          because my humble self must be the first
          to exhibit that obedience.
SEG.:   You are Clotaldo. Then, how is it
          that the man who mistreats me in prison
          treats me with such respect?
          What's going on here with me?
CLO.:   In the great confusion
          that your new condition causes you,
          your mind and reason
          will suffer a thousand doubts;
            but I now wish to rid you
          of all of them (if possible),
          because, Sire, you ought to know
          that you are crown prince
            of Poland. If you have lived
          in hiding and retirement,
          it was in obedience
          to the severity of fate,
            which promises a thousand disasters
          to this realm at such time
          as the laurel of sovereignty
          wreathes your noble brow here.
            But, in the firm belief that your good sense
          will make you cancel the planets' decree—

porque es posible vencellas
a un magnánimo varón,
   a palacio te han traído
de la torre en que vivías,
mientras al sueño tenías
el espíritu rendido.
   Tu padre, el rey mi señor,
vendrá a verte, y de él sabrás,
Segismundo, lo demás.

SEG.: ¡Pues, vil, infame y traidor!
   ¿qué tengo más que saber,
después de saber quién soy
para mostrar desde hoy
mi soberbia y mi poder?
   ¿Cómo a tu patria le has hecho
tal traición, que me ocultaste
a mí, pues que me negaste,
contra razón y derecho,
   este estado?

CLO.:   ¡Ay de mí triste!

SEG.: Traidor fuiste con la ley,
lisonjero con el rey,
y cruel conmigo fuiste;
   y así el rey, la ley y yo,
entre desdichas tan fieras,
te condenan a que mueras
a mis manos.

CRI. 2.º: ¡Señor!

SEG.:   No
   me estorbe nadie, que es vana
diligencia; ¡y vive Dios!
si os ponéis delante vos,
que os eche por la ventana.

CRI. 1.º: Huye, Clotaldo.

CLO.:   ¡Ay de ti,
   qué soberbia vas mostrando,
sin saber que estás soñando!   (Vase.)

CRI. 2.º: Advierte . . .

SEG.:   Apartad de aquí.

CRI. 2.º: que a su rey obedeció.

SEG.:   En lo que no es justa ley

因为 because a highminded man
can resist them—
you have been brought to the palace
from the tower in which you were dwelling
while your spirits
were overcome by sleep.
Your father, my lord the King,
will come to see you, and from him you will learn
the rest, Segismundo.

SEG.: So, you base, vile traitor!
What more do I need to learn,
after learning who I am,
in order to demonstrate my pride
and power from now on?
How could you commit such treason
against your country as to hide me
away, since, against all reason
and justice, you were robbing me
of this rank in life?

CLO.:   Oh, woe is me!

SEG.: You were a traitor to the law,
a flatterer to the king,
and cruel to me;
and so, the king, the law, and I,
amid such grievous misfortunes,
condemn you to death
at my hands.

SER. 2:   Sire!

SEG.:   Let
no one prevent me, for it would be wasted
effort; and, as God lives,
if you interpose,
I'll throw you out the window!

SER. 1: Escape, Clotaldo!

CLO.:   Alas for you!
What pride you're displaying,
unaware that you're only dreaming!   (*Exit.*)

SER. 2: Please observe . . .

SEG.:   Get out of here!

SER. 2: . . . that he was merely obeying his king.

SEG.: In matters that violate the law

no ha de obedecer al rey,
y su príncipe era yo.

CRI. 2.º: El no debió examinar
si era bien hecho o mal hecho.

SEG.:   Que estáis mal con vos sospecho,
pues me dais que replicar.

CLA.:   Dice el príncipe muy bien,
y vos hicistes muy mal.

CRI. 2.º: ¿Quién os dio licencia igual?

CLA.:   Yo me la he tomado.

SEG.:   ¿Quién
eres tú, di?

CLA.:   Entremetido
y de este oficio soy jefe,
porque soy el mequetrefe
mayor que se ha conocido.

SEG.:   Tú sólo en tan nuevos mundos
me has agradado.

CLA.:   Señor,
soy un grande agradador
de todos los Segismundos.

Sale ASTOLFO.

AST.:   ¡Feliz mil veces el día,
oh Príncipe, que os mostráis
sol de Polonia y llenáis
de resplandor y alegría
todos estos horizontes
con tan divino arrebol,
pues que salís como el sol
de debajo de los montes!
Salid, pues, y aunque tan tarde
se corona vuestra frente
del laurel resplandeciente,
tarde muera.

SEG.:   Dios os guarde.

AST.:   El no haberme conocido
sólo por disculpa os doy

the king doesn't have to be obeyed,
and, after all, I was his prince.

SER. 2: It wasn't for him to inquire
whether the actions were proper or not.

SEG.: I suspect that you're your own worst enemy
for forcing me to talk back to you.

CLA.: The Prince is perfectly right,
and you behaved very badly.

SER. 2: Who gave you permission to speak?

CLA.: I took it upon myself.

SEG.: Tell me,
who are you?

CLA.: A busybody,
and a master at my trade,
because I'm the nosiest
person ever known.

SEG.: Of all these people new to me, you alone
have pleased me.

CLA.: Sire,
I am a great pleaser
of all Segismundos.[16]

Enter ASTOLFO.

AST.: A thousand times happy the day,
O Prince, when you show yourself
as the sun of Poland, filling
with splendor and joy
all these horizons
with such a divine red glow,
since you emerge like the sun
from below the mountains!
Emerge, then, and even though your brow
is wreathed so belatedly
with the glorious laurel,
may it be equally slow to die!

SEG.: God keep you.

AST.: Your failure to recognize me
is the only excuse I make for you

16. At least one commentator believes this may be an allusion to the three historical kings of Poland named Sigismund (they reigned between 1506 and 1632). Clarín
would have pleased them because they were all warlike, and he is a "clarion."

de no honrarme más. Yo soy
Astolfo, duque he nacido
de Moscovia, y primo vuestro;
haya igualdad en los dos.

SEG.: Si digo que os guarde Dios,
¿bastante agrado no os muestro?
Pero ya que, haciendo alarde
de quien sois, de osto os quejáis,
otra vez que me veáis
le diré a Dios que no os guarde.

CRI. 2.°: Vuestra Alteza considere
que como en montes nacido
con todos ha procedido.
Astolfo, señor, prefiere . . .

SEG.: Cansóme como llegó
grave a hablarme, y lo primero
que hizo, se puso el sombrero.

CRI. 2.°: Es grande.

SEG.: Mayor soy yo.

CRI. 2.°: Con todo eso, entre los dos
que haya más respeto es bien
que entre los demás.

SEG.: ¿Y quién
os mete conmigo a vos?

Sale ESTRELLA.

EST.: Vuestra Alteza, señor, sea
muchas veces bien venido
al dosel que, agradecido,
le recibe y le desea,
adonde, a pesar de engaños,
viva augusto y eminente,
donde su vida se cuente
por siglos, y no por años.

SEG.: Dime tú ahora ¿quién es
esta beldad soberana?
¿Quién es esta diosa humana,
a cuyos divinos pies
postra el cielo su arrebol?
¿Quién es esta mujer bella?

CLA.: Es, señor, tu prima Estrella.

for not showing me greater respect. I am
Astolfo, and I was born duke
  of Muscovy, and your cousin;
let us stand on equal terms.

SEG.: If I say "God keep you,"
am I not satisfying you?
  But now that, boasting
about who you are, you complain about it,
the next time you see me
I'll ask God *not* to keep you.

SER. 2: Your Highness should take into account
that, since he was born in the hills,
he has behaved that way with everyone.
My lord, Astolfo prefers . . .

SEG.: He peeved me the way he happened
to speak to me so stuffily, and the first thing
he did was to put on his hat in front of me.

SER. 2: He's a grandee.

SEG.:   I am grander yet.

SER. 2: However that may be, it's only proper
that there should be greater respect between you two
than between anyone else.

SEG.:   And who
asked you to meddle in my business?

Enter ESTRELLA.

EST.: Sire, may Your Highness be
welcomed many times
to the throne that gratefully
receives and desires you,
  and where, in spite of deceit,
may you live revered and eminent,
your life being reckoned
in centuries, not years!

SEG.: Tell me now, who is
this peerless beauty?
Who is this human goddess
at whose divine feet
  heaven prostrates its glow?
Who is this beautiful woman?

CLA.: Sire, it's your cousin Estrella—"Star."

SEG.:   Mejor dijeras el sol.
         Aunque el parabién es bien
         darme del bien que conquisto,
         de sólo haberos hoy visto
         os admito el parabién;
             y así, del llegarme a ver
         con el bien que no merezco,
         el parabién agradezco,
         Estrella, que amanecer
             podéis, y dar alegría
         al más luciente farol.
             ¿Qué dejáis que hacer al sol,
         si os levantáis con el día?
             Dadme a besar vuestra mano
         en cuya copa de nieve
         el aura candores bebe.
EST.:   Sed más galán cortesano.
AST.:   Si él toma la mano, yo
         soy perdido.
CRI. 2.°:   El pesar sé
         de Astolfo, y le estorbaré.
         Advierte, señor, que no
             es justo atreverse así,
         y estando Astolfo . . .
SEG.:   ¿No digo
         que vos no os metáis conmigo?
CRI. 2.°: Digo lo que es justo.
SEG.:   A mí
         todo eso me causa enfado.
         Nada me parece justo
         en siendo contra mi gusto.
CRI. 2.°: Pues yo, señor, he escuchado
             de ti que en lo justo es bien
         obedecer y servir.
SEG.:   También oíste decir
             que por un balcón a quien
             me canse sabré arrojar.
CRI. 2.°: Con los hombres como yo
         no puede hacerse eso.
SEG.:   ¿No?
         ¡Por Dios, que lo he de probar!

SEG.:   You should have said: the sun.
      Though it's fitting to congratulate me
on the good fortune I have obtained,
it is only because I have seen you today
that I accept your congratulations;
      and so, because I find myself in possession
of good fortune that I don't deserve,
I thank you for the congratulations,
Estrella, you star that are able
      to appear at dawn and bring joy
to the brightest heavenly lamp.
What work do you leave for the sun to do
if you rise with the day?
      Allow me to kiss your hand,
from whose snowy goblet
the air drinks whiteness.

EST.:   Be a more refined courtier.

AST.:   If he takes her hand, I
am ruined.

SER. 2:   I know how grieved
Astolfo feels, and I'll prevent this.
Sire, take note that it isn't
   right to be so forward,
especially when Astolfo is . . .

SEG.:   Didn't I tell you
not to meddle in my business?

SER. 2: I'm only saying what's right.

SEG.:   As for me,
all of this is making me angry.
Nothing seems right to me
if it goes against my grain.

SER. 2: But I, Sire, have heard
   you say that it's proper to follow righteousness
when obeying and serving.

SEG.:   You've also heard me say
that I'm capable of hurling from a balcony
   anyone who nags at me.

SER. 2: That can't be done
to men of my station.

SEG.:   Oh, no?
By God, I've got to try it out!

Cógele en los brazos, y éntrase, y todos tras él,
y torna a salir.

AST.:   ¿Qué es esto que llego a ver?
EST.:   ¡Llegad todos a ayudar!   (*Vase.*)
SEG.:   Cayó del balcón al mar;
            ¡vive Dios, que pudo ser!
AST.:   Pues medid con más espacio
            vuestras acciones severas,
            que lo que hay de hombres a fieras,
            hay desde un monte a palacio.
SEG.:   Pues en dando tan severo
            en hablar con entereza,
            quizá no hallaréis cabeza
            en que se os tenga el sombrero.

            Vase ASTOLFO *y sale el* REY.

BAS.:   ¿Qué ha sido esto?
SEG.:   Nada ha sido;
            a un hombre, que me ha cansado,
            de ese balcón he arrojado.
CLA.:   Que es el rey, está advertido.
BAS.:   ¿Tan presto una vida cuesta
            tu venida el primer día?
SEG.:   Díjome que no podía
            hacerse, y gané la apuesta.
BAS.:   Pésame mucho que cuando,
            príncipe, a verte he venido,
            pensando hallarte advertido,
            de hados y estrellas triunfando,
            con tanto rigor te vea,
            y que la primera acción
            que has hecho en esta ocasión,
            un grave homicidio sea.
            ¿Con qué amor llegar podré
            a darte ahora mis brazos,
            si de sus soberbios lazos,
            que están enseñados sé
            a dar muertes? ¿Quién llegó

He seizes him in his arms and exits, with everyone following,
then enters again.

AST.:   What did I just see?

EST.:   Everyone, come help!   (*Exit.*)

SEG.:   He fell from the balcony into the sea;[17]
as God lives, it *was* possible!

AST.:   Please reflect more calmly
on your drastic actions,
because just as great as the gulf between man and beast
is the gulf between mountain and palace.

SEG.:   Well, if you persist so drastically
in speaking from your heart,
maybe you won't find a head
to perch that hat of yours on!

Exit ASTOLFO. *Enter King* BASILIO.

BAS.:   What's been going on here?

SEG.:   Nothing;
a fellow annoyed me
and I threw him from that balcony.

CLA.:   Be warned: it's the King!

BAS.:   On the very first day, your coming
costs a life so soon?

SEG.:   He told me it couldn't
be done, and I won the bet.

BAS.:   I'm very sorry, Prince,
that, on my coming to see you,
thinking I'd find you forewarned
and triumphing over your fate and planets,
I should see you behaving so violently,
and that the first deed
you have done on this occasion
should be a dire murder.
How can I now go to you lovingly
and offer you my arms,
when I know that your prideful embrace
has learned how
to kill? Who has ever

---

17. Some editors, concerned about the historical boundaries of Poland, take *mar*
here to mean a pond.

a ver desnudo el puñal
que dio una herida mortal,
que no temiese? ¿Quién vio
    sangriento el lugar, adonde
a otro hombre dieron muerte,
que no sienta?, que el más fuerte
a su natural responde.
    Yo así, que en tus brazos miro
de esta muerte el instrumento,
y miro el lugar sangriento,
de tus brazos me retiro;
    y aunque en amorosos lazos
ceñir tu cuello pensé,
sin ellos me volveré,
que tengo miedo a tus brazos.

SEG.:   Sin ellos me podré estar
como me he estado hasta aquí;
que un padre que contra mí
tanto rigor sabe usar,
    que con condición ingrata
de su lado me desvía,
como a una fiera me cría,
y como a un monstruo me trata
    y mi muerte solicita,
de poca importancia fue
que los brazos no me dé
cuando el ser de hombre me quita.

BAS.:   Al cielo y a Dios pluguiera
que a dártele no llegara;
pues ni tu voz escuchara,
ni tu atrevimiento viera.

SEG.:   Si no me le hubieras dado,
no me quejara de ti;
pero una vez dado, sí,
por habérmele quitado;
    que aunque el dar el acción es
más noble y más singular,
es mayor bajeza el dar,
para quitarlo después.

BAS.:   ¡Bien me agradeces el verte,
de un humilde y pobre preso,

seen unsheathed the dagger
that dealt a mortal blow,
and not been afraid? Who has seen
   the bloodstained place where
one man has killed another,
and not felt grief?—for even the strongest man
yields to his human nature.
   And so, seeing that your arms
were the instrument of this death,
and gazing on the bloodstained place,
I withdraw from your arms;
   and, even though I intended to circle
your neck in a loving embrace,
I shall go away without it
because I fear your arms.

SEG.:   I can get along without it
just as I've done up till now;
because when a father is capable of showing
such severity to me
   that he thrusts me from his side
into an unpleasant way of life,
raising me like a wild animal,
treating me like a monster,
   and seeking my death,
it hardly matters at all
that he refuses to embrace me
after he has deprived me of human status.

BAS.:   I wish it had pleased God and heaven
that I had never given you life at all;
then, I wouldn't have heard your voice
or seen your rashness.

SEG.:   If you had never given it to me at all,
I'd have no complaint against you;
but, since you did, I do:
for having deprived me of it;
   because, whereas giving is
the noblest, most outstanding thing a man can do,
it's all the more despicable to give
and then take back the gift.

BAS.:   It's a fine way you have of thanking me for finding yourself
changed from a humble, poor prisoner

príncipe ya!

SEG.:   Pues en eso
¿qué tengo que agradecerte?
Tirano de mi albedrío,
si viejo y caduco estás,
muriéndote, ¿qué me das?
¿Dasme más de lo que es mío?
Mi padre eres y mi rey;
luego toda esta grandeza
me da la naturaleza
por derechos de su ley.
    Luego aunque esté en este estado,
obligado no te quedo,
y pedirte cuentas puedo
del tiempo que me has quitado
    libertad, vida y honor;
y así, agradéceme a mí
que yo no cobre de ti,
pues eres tú mi deudor.

BAS.:   Bárbaro eres y atrevido:
cumplió su palabra el cielo;
y así, para él mismo apelo:
soberbio y desvanecido.
    Y aunque sepas ya quién eres,
y desengañado estés,
y aunque en un lugar te ves
donde a todos te prefieres,
    mira bien lo que te advierto,
que seas humilde y blando,
porque quizá estás soñando,
aunque ves que estás despierto.   (Vase.)

SEG.:   ¿Que quizá soñando estoy,
aunque despierto me veo?
No sueño, pues toco y creo
lo que he sido y lo que soy.
    Y aunque ahora te arrepientas,
poco remedio tendrás:
sé quien soy, y no podrás,
aunque suspires y sientas,
    quitarme el haber nacido
de esta corona heredero;

into a prince!

SEG.:   Well, for all that
why should I thank you?
     You tyrant over my free will,
if you're old and feeble,
what will you give me when you die?
Will you give me any more than what's coming to me?
     You're my father and my king;
so that all this grandeur
is given to me by Nature
in accordance with her laws.
     Thus, even if I now have this rank,
I'm not obliged to you for it,
and I can ask you for a reckoning
of the time during which you deprived me
     of freedom, life, and honor;
and so, *you* should thank *me*
for not trying to collect from you,
since you're in my debt.

BAS.:   You're an insolent barbarian:
heaven has kept its word;
and so, it is to heaven that I appeal,
you prideful, conceited man!
     And, even though you now know who you are,
and the delusion has been lifted from you,
and you find yourself in a place
where you take precedence over all others,
     pay close heed to my admonition
to be humble and tractable,
because you may be just dreaming,
even though you think you're awake!   (*Exit.*)

SEG.:   I may be just dreaming,
even though I think I'm awake?
I'm not dreaming, because I feel and believe
that which I was and that which I am.
     And, even though you regret it now,
there's not much you can do about it:
I know who I am, and even if you sigh
and grieve, you won't be able
     to undo the fact that I was born
heir to this crown;

y si me viste primero
a las prisiones rendido,
    fue porque ignoré quién era;
pero ya informado estoy
de quién soy, y sé que soy
un compuesto de hombre y fiera.

Sale ROSAURA, *dama.*

ROS.:   Siguiendo a Estrella vengo,
y gran temor de hallar a Astolfo tengo;
    que Clotaldo desea
que no sepa quién soy, y no me vea,
    porque dice que importa al honor mío;
y de Clotaldo fío
    su efeto, pues le debo agradecida
aquí el amparo de mi honor y vida.
CLA.:   ¿Qué es lo que te ha agradado
más de cuanto hoy has visto y admirado?
SEG.:   Nada me ha suspendido,
que todo lo tenía prevenido;
    mas, si admirar hubiera
algo en el mundo, la hermosura fuera
de la mujer. Leía
una vez en los libros que tenía,
    que lo que a Dios mayor estudio debe
era el hombre, por ser un mundo breve;
    mas ya que lo es recelo
la mujer, pues ha sido un breve cielo,
    y más beldad encierra
que el hombre, cuanto va de cielo a tierra;
    y más si es la que miro.
ROS.:   El príncipe está aquí; yo me retiro.
SEG.:   Oye, mujer, detente;
no juntes el ocaso y el oriente,
    huyendo al primer paso;
que juntos el oriente y el ocaso,
    la lumbre y sombra fría,
serás sin duda síncopa del día.
    Pero ¿qué es lo que veo?
ROS.:   Lo mismo que estoy viendo dudo y creo.
SEG.:   Yo he visto esta belleza

and if you saw me formerly
a prisoner of my shackles,
   it was because I didn't know who I was;
but now I have been informed
as to who I am, and I know that I'm
a hybrid of man and beast.

Enter ROSAURA, *attired as a lady-in-waiting.*

ROS.:   I come here in Estrella's train,
and I mightily fear meeting Astolfo;
   because it is Clotaldo's wish
that he not know who I am, and not see me,
   because he says it's essential to my honor;
and I'm trusting Clotaldo with the
   results, since I thankfully owe to him
the protection of my honor and life here.

CLA.:   What has given you the most pleasure
of everything you have seen and wondered at today?

SEG.:   Nothing dumbfounded me,
because I had foreseen it all;
   but, if I were to wonder at
anything in the world, it would be the beauty
of woman. I read
once in the books that I had
   that the creation that cost God the greatest effort
was man, because he is a world in miniature;
   but now I suspect that it was
woman, since she has become a heaven in miniature,
   and contains as much more beauty
than man as the difference between heaven and earth;
   and even more, if she's the one I now espy.

ROS.:   The prince is here; I shall withdraw.

SEG.:   Listen, woman, stop where you are;
don't let sunset follow immediately upon sunrise
   by escaping after your first step;
because, when sunrise and sunset are joined,
   the light with the cold darkness,
you will no doubt cause the day to be telescoped.
   But what's this I see?

ROS.:   I both doubt and believe what I'm seeing.

SEG.:   I have seen this beauty

<table>
<tr><td></td><td>otra vez.</td></tr>
</table>

ROS.:   Yo esta pompa, esta grandeza
    he visto reducida
    a una estrecha prisión.

SEG.:   Ya hallé mi vida;
    mujer, que aqueste nombre
    es el mejor requiebro para el hombre:
    ¿quién eres? Que sin verte
    adoración me debes, y de suerte
    por la fe te conquisto,
    que me persuado a que otra vez te he visto.
    ¿Quién eres, mujer bella?

ROS.:   (Disimular me importa.) Soy de Estrella
    una infelice dama.

SEG.:   No digas tal, di el sol, a cuya llama
    aquella estrella vive,
    pues de tus rayos resplandor recibe;
    yo vi, en reino de olores,
    que presidía entre comunes flores
    la deidad de la rosa,
    y era su emperatriz por más hermosa.
    Yo vi entre piedras finas
    de la docta academia de sus minas
    preferir el diamante,
    y ser su emperador por más brillante.
    Yo en esas cortes bellas
    de la inquieta república de estrellas,
    vi en el lugar primero,
    por rey de las estrellas el lucero.
    Yo en esferas perfetas
    llamando el sol a cortes los planetas,
    le vi que presidía,
    como mayor oráculo del día.
    Pues ¿cómo si entre estrellas,
    piedras, planetas, flores, las más bellas
    prefieren, tú has servido
    la de menos beldad habiendo sido
    por más bella y hermosa,
    sol, lucero, diamante, estrella y rosa?

before.

ROS.:　　　　I have seen this pomp, this
　　　grandeur locked up
　　　in a cramped prison.

SEG.:　　　　　　　　　Now I have found my life;
　　　woman (for that name
　　　is the greatest compliment a man can pay):
　　　who are you? Because, though I haven't seen you,
　　　you owe me thanks for worshipping you, and I
　　　　recognize you by some strong conviction,[18] so that
　　　I'm sure I've seen you before.
　　　Who are you, beautiful woman?

ROS.:　　(I must dissemble!) I am an unhappy
　　　lady-in-waiting of Estrella's.

SEG.:　　Don't say that, say: the sun, from whose flame
　　　that Estrella-star lives,
　　　since she receives splendor from your beams;
　　　　in the realm of fragrances, I have seen
　　　the divine rose
　　　　presiding over the common flowers
　　　as their empress because of her greater beauty.
　　　　Among precious stones, I have seen
　　　the learned academy of their mines
　　　　prefer the diamond,
　　　named their emperor because of its greater brilliance.
　　　　In that beautiful parliament
　　　of the inconstant commonwealth of the stars,
　　　　I saw in first place,
　　　as king of the stars, the evening star.
　　　　When, amid the sublime orbits,
　　　the sun summoned the planets to a parliament,
　　　　I saw him taking precedence,
　　　since he was the chief oracle of the day.
　　　　Then, seeing that among the stars,
　　　stones, planets, and flowers the most beautiful
　　　　are preferred, how is it that you have come to serve
　　　a woman of lesser beauty, while you,
　　　　as the more beautiful and lovely one, are the
　　　sun, evening star, diamond, star, and rose?

---

18. This phrase has also been interpreted differently.

Sale CLOTALDO.

CLO.:   A Segismundo reducir deseo,
              porque en fin le he criado; mas ¿qué veo?
ROS.:   Tu favor reverencio:
              respóndate retórico el silencio;
              cuando tan torpe la razón se halla,
              mejor habla, señor, quien mejor calla.
SEG.:   No has de ausentarte, espera.
              ¿Cómo quieres dejar desa manera
              a oscuras mi sentido?
ROS.:   Esta licencia a Vuestra Alteza pido.
SEG.:   Irte con tal violencia
              no es pedir, es tomarte la licencia.
ROS.:   Pues si tú no la das, tomarla espero.
SEG.:   Harás que de cortés pase a grosero,
              porque la resistencia
              es veneno cruel de mi paciencia.
ROS.:   Pues cuando ese veneno,
              de furia, de rigor y saña lleno,
              la paciencia venciera,
              mi respeto no osara, ni pudiera.
SEG.:   Sólo por ver si puedo,
              harás que pierda a tu hermosura el miedo,
              que soy muy inclinado
              a vencer lo imposible; hoy he arrojado
              de ese balcón a un hombre, que decía
              que hacerse no podía;
              y así por ver si puedo, cosa es llana
              que arrojaré tu honor por la ventana.
CLO.:   Mucho se va empeñando.
              ¿Qué he de hacer, cielos, cuando
              tras un loco deseo
              mi honor segunda vez a riesgo veo?
ROS.:   No en vano prevenía
              a este reino infeliz tu tiranía
              escándalos tan fuertes
              de delitos, traiciones, iras, muertes.
              Mas ¿qué ha de hacer un hombre,
              que no tiene de humano más que el nombre,
              atrevido, inhumano,

Enter CLOTALDO.

CLO.:   I wish to pacify Segismundo,
          because, after all, I raised him; but what's this I see?
ROS.:   I venerate your kindness:
          let my silence be an eloquent reply;
              when reason is so sluggish,
          Sire, the best speaker is the one who is most silent.
SEG.:   You may not withdraw! Wait!
          How can you wish to leave
              my mind in the dark this way?
ROS.:   I request of Your Highness permission to go.
SEG.:   To leave so impetuously
          is not asking for permission but seizing it.
ROS.:   Well, if you won't grant it, I hope to seize it.
SEG.:   You'll make me change from courteous to coarse,
              because resistance
          is a bitter poison to my patience.
ROS.:   Well, even if that poison,
          filled with fury, harshness, and rage,
              should overcome your patience,
          it wouldn't dare—it couldn't—overcome your respect for me.
SEG.:   Merely to see whether I can do it,
          you'll make me lose my fear for your beauty,
              because I'm greatly inclined
          to perform the impossible; today I threw
          from that balcony a man who said
          it couldn't be done;
              and so, to see whether I can, it's a simple thing
          for me to throw your honor out the window.
CLO.:   He's pressing her very hard!
          Heavens, what am I to do, when
              I see a mad desire
          setting my honor at risk once again?
ROS.:   It wasn't for nothing that it was predicted
          your tyranny would bring this unhappy kingdom
              such heavy shocks
          of crime, deception, wrath, and death.
          But what can a man be expected to do
          who has nothing human about him except the name,
              who is insolent, inhuman,

cruel, soberbio, bárbaro y tirano,
nacido entre las fieras?

SEG.:   Porque tú ese baldón no me dijeras,
tan cortés me mostraba,
pensando que con eso te obligaba;
mas si lo soy hablando de este modo,
has de decirlo, vive Dios, por todo.
—Hola, dejadnos solos, y esa puerta
se cierre, y no entre nadie.

Vase CLARÍN.

ROS.:   Yo soy muerta.
Advierte . . .
SEG.:   Soy tirano,
y ya pretendes reducirme en vano.
CLO.:   ¡Oh, qué lance tan fuerte!
Saldré a estorbarlo, aunque me dé la muerte.
Señor, atiende, mira.
SEG.:   Segunda vez me has provocado a ira,
viejo caduco y loco.
¿Mi enojo y mi rigor tienes en poco?
¿Cómo hasta aquí has llegado?
CLO.:   De los acentos de esta voz llamado,
a decirte que seas
más apacible, si reinar deseas:
y no por verte ya de todos dueño,
seas cruel, porque quizá es un sueño.
SEG.:   A rabia me provocas,
cuando la luz del desengaño tocas.
Veré, dándote muerte,
si es sueño o si verdad.

Al ir a sacar la daga se la detiene CLOTALDO,
y se arrodilla.

CLO.:   Yo de esta suerte
librar mi vida espero.
SEG.:   Quita la osada mano del acero.
CLO.:   Hasta que gente venga
que tu rigor y cólera detenga,
no he de soltarte.
ROS.:   ¡Ay cielos!

cruel, prideful, barbarous, and tyrannical,
born amid wild beasts?

SEG.: It was to prevent you from insulting me like this
that I showed so much courtesy,
thinking I would find favor with you that way;
But if, even after speaking politely, I am still such a monster,
as God lives, I'll make you say it for every reason!
—You there, leave us alone, and let that door
be locked, and let no one come in!

Exit CLARÍN.

ROS.:   I'm as good as dead!
Please observe . . .

SEG.:   I'm a tyrant,
and by now it's no use trying to pacify me.

CLO.: Oh, what a terrible moment!
I'll go out and prevent him, even if he kills me.
Sire, wait, think of what you're doing!

SEG.: Once again you have aroused my wrath,
feeble, crazy old man.
Have you so little regard for my vexation and my severity?
How is it that you got all the way here?

CLO.: I was summoned by the sound of your voice,
to tell you to be
more even-tempered, if you wish to be king:
and not to be cruel just because you now find yourself
master of us all, because it may be a dream.

SEG.: You drive me to frenzy
when you mention the light of disillusionment.
By killing you, I'll see
whether it's a dream or reality.

As he is about to draw his dagger,
CLOTALDO *stays his hand and kneels.*

CLO.:   In this fashion
I hope to save my life.

SEG.: Take your rash hand off my steel!

CLO.:   Until people come
to restrain your harsh anger,
I won't let go of you.

ROS.:   Oh, heavens!

SEG.:   Suelta, digo,
caduco loco, bárbaro enemigo,
o será de esta suerte   (*Luchan.*)
el darte ahora entre mis brazos muerte.
ROS.:   Acudid todos, presto,
que matan a Clotaldo.   (*Vase.*)

Sale ASTOLFO *a tiempo que cae* CLOTALDO *a sus pies,*
y él se pone en medio.

AST.:   ¿Pues qué es esto,
príncipe generoso?
¿Así se mancha acero tan brioso
en una sangre helada?
Vuelva a la vaina tu lucida espada.
SEG.:   En viéndola teñida
en esa infame sangre.
AST.:   Ya su vida
tomó a mis pies sagrado,
y de algo ha de servirme haber llegado.
SEG.:   Sírvate de morir; pues de esta suerte
también sabré vengarme con tu muerte
de aquel pasado enojo.
AST.:   Yo defiendo
mi vida; así la majestad no ofendo.

Sacan las espadas, y sale el REY BASILIO, *y* ESTRELLA.

CLO.:   No le ofendas, señor.
BAS.:   ¿Pues aquí espadas?
EST.:   ¡Astolfo es, ay de mí, penas airadas!
BAS.:   ¿Pues qué es lo que ha pasado?
AST.:   Nada, señor, habiendo tú llegado.
                                          (*Envainan.*)
SEG.:   Mucho, señor, aunque hayas tú venido;
yo a ese viejo matar he pretendido.
BAS.:   ¿Respeto no tenías
a estas canas?
CLO.:   Señor, ved que son mías;
que no importa veréis.
SEG.:   Acciones vanas,
querer que tenga yo respeto a canas;
pues aún ésas podría

SEG.:   Let go, I say,
        feeble madman, barbarous enemy,
        [*as they struggle:*] or this will be the way
        I will now kill you with my embrace.
ROS.:   Everyone come running quickly,
        Clotaldo is being killed!   (*Exit.*)

        ASTOLFO *enters just as* CLOTALDO *falls at his feet,*
                and he interposes.

AST.:   Why, what's this,
        noble Prince?
        Is this how such a vigorous blade is stained
        with the chilled blood of an old man?
        Return your gleaming sword to its sheath.
SEG.:   Not till I see it dyed
        in his base blood!
AST.:   His life has already
        claimed sanctuary at my feet,
        and my arrival must have some effect.
SEG.:   Let it have the effect of your death; because that way
        I'll also be able to take revenge, by killing you,
        for that earlier vexation.
AST.:   I am fighting
        in self-defense, and thus not affronting the royal person.

        They draw their swords. Enter King BASILIO *and* ESTRELLA.

CLO.:   Don't harm him, my lord!
BAS.:   What, drawn swords here?
EST.:   It's Astolfo, woe is me, what awful grief!
BAS.:   Well, what's happened?
AST.:   Nothing, Sire, now that *you* have come.
                                (*They sheathe their swords.*)
SEG.:   A great deal, Sire, even if you have come;
        I tried to kill this old man.
BAS.:   You had no respect
        for his gray hair?
CLO.:   Sire, consider that the hair is only mine,
        and you'll see it's of no importance.
SEG.:   A vain effort,
        to want me to respect gray hair;
        for even yours, perhaps,

ser que viese a mis plantas algún día,
porque aún no estoy vengado
del modo injusto con que me has criado.   (*Vase.*)

BAS.:   Pues antes que lo veas,
volverás a dormir adonde creas
que cuanto te ha pasado,
como fue bien del mundo, fue soñado.

Vase el REY, *y* CLOTALDO.
Quedan ESTRELLA, *y* ASTOLFO.

AST.:   ¡Qué pocas veces el hado
que dice desdichas, miente!
pues es tan cierto en los males,
como dudoso en los bienes.
¡Qué buen astrólogo fuera
si siempre casos crueles
anunciara, pues no hay duda
que ellos fueran verdad siempre!
Conocerse esta experiencia
en mí y Segismundo puede,
Estrella, pues en los dos
hizo muestras diferentes.
En él previno rigores,
soberbias, desdichas, muertes,
y en todo dijo verdad,
porque todo, al fin, sucede.
Pero en mí, que al ver, señora,
esos rayos excelentes,
de quien el sol fue una sombra
y el cielo un amago breve,
que me previno venturas,
trofeos, aplausos, bienes,
dijo mal, y dijo bien;
pues sólo es justo que acierte
cuando amaga con favores
y ejecuta con desdenes.

EST.:   No dudo que esas finezas
son verdades evidentes;
mas serán por otra dama,
cuyo retrato pendiente
trajisteis al cuello cuando

I may see at my feet some day,
   because I still haven't taken revenge
for the unfair way in which you raised me!   (*Exit.*)

BAS.:   Well, before you see such a sight,
you'll go back to sleep, and you'll believe
   that everything that has happened to you,
since it entailed worldly goods, was just a dream.

Exit King BASILIO *and* CLOTALDO.
ESTRELLA *and* ASTOLFO *remain.*

AST.:   How seldom a destiny
that predicts misfortune lies!
Because it's just as accurate with regard to bad things
as it is uncertain with regard to the good.
What a wonderful astrologer I would be
if I always foretold dire
events, because there's no doubt
they would always come to pass!
This conclusion can be demonstrated
in the case of Segismundo and me,
Estrella, since in the two of us
it showed different aspects.
To him were foretold harshness,
pridefulness, misfortunes, and murders,
and it all was true,
because it's finally happening.
But in my case, my lady, I who saw
your bright beams,
to which the sun was a mere shadow
and heaven an inadequate hint,
when fate promised me good fortune,
triumphs, acclaim, and good things,
it was both wrong and right;
because it can only be correct
when it hints at benefits
and delivers disdain.

EST.:   I have no doubt that those compliments
are shining truths;
but they must be meant for another lady,
whose pendant portrait
you wore on your neck when

llegasteis, Astolfo, a verme;
y siendo así, esos requiebros
ella sola los merece.
Acudid a que ella os pague,
que no son buenos papeles
en el consejo de amor
las finezas ni las fees
que se hicieron en servicio
de otras damas y otros reyes.

                    Sale ROSAURA *al paño.*

ROS.:   ¡Gracias a Dios que han llegado
        ya mis desdichas crueles
        al término suyo, pues
        quien esto ve nada teme!
AST.:   Yo haré que el retrato salga
        del pecho, para que entre
        la imagen de tu hermosura.
        Donde entra Estrella no tiene
        lugar la sombra, ni estrella
        donde el sol; voy a traerle.
        perdona, Rosaura hermosa,   *(Aparte.)*
        este agravio, porque ausentes,
        no se guardan más fe que ésta
        los hombres y las mujeres.   *(Vase.)*
ROS.:   Nada he podido escuchar,
        temerosa que me viese.
EST.:   ¡Astrea!
ROS.:   Señora mía.
EST.:   Heme holgado que tú fueses
        la que llegaste hasta aquí;
        porque de ti solamente
        fiara un secreto.
ROS.:   Honras,
        señora, a quien te obedece.
EST.:   En el poco tiempo, Astrea,
        que ha que te conozco, tienes
        de mi voluntad las llaves;
        por esto, y por ser quien eres,
        me atrevo a fiar de ti
        lo que aún de mí muchas veces

you came to see me, Astolfo;
and, that being the case, she alone
deserves your verbal bouquets.
See to it that she repays you for them,
because in Love's tribunal
the compliments and vows
made in the service
of other ladies and other rulers
aren't valid documents.

ROSAURA *enters unnoticed.*

ROS.:   Thank God that my cruel
misfortunes have now reached
their limit—because
whoever has seen this, has nothing left to fear!

AST.:   I'll see to it that the portrait leaves
my breast, so that the image
of your beauty can enter into it.
Wherever Estrella enters, there is
no place for shadow, just as no star remains
after sunrise; I'm going to fetch it.
(*Aside:*) Forgive me, lovely Rosaura,
for this affront, because, when they are apart,
men and women
are no more faithful than this!   (*Exit.*)

ROS.:   I wasn't able to hear anything,
I was so afraid of his seeing me.

EST.:   Astraea!

ROS.:   My lady?

EST.:   I'm very pleased that it was you
who followed me all the way here;
because to you alone
I'd entrust a secret.

ROS.:   My lady,
you honor the one who obeys you.

EST.:   Astraea, in the short while
that I've known you, you've won
the keys to my private thoughts;
for that reason, and because of the kind of person you are,
I venture to admit to you
something that I've concealed even from myself

recaté.
ROS.:   Tu esclava soy.
EST.:   Pues para decirlo en breve,
          mi primo Astolfo (bastara
          que mi primo te dijese,
          porque hay cosas que se dicen
          con pensarlas solamente),
          ha de casarse conmigo,
          si es que la fortuna quiere
          que con una dicha sola
          tantas desdichas descuente.
          Pesóme que el primer día
          echado al cuello trajese
          el retrato de una dama;
          habléle en él cortésmente,
          es galán, y quiere bien;
          fue por él, y ha de traerle
          aquí; embarázame mucho
          que él a mí a dármele llegue:
          quédate aquí, y cuando venga,
          le dirás que te le entregue
          a ti. No te digo más;
          discreta y hermosa eres,
          bien sabrás lo que es amor.   (*Vase.*)
ROS.:   ¡Ojalá no lo supiese!
          ¡Válgame el cielo! ¿quién fuera
          tan atenta y tan prudente,
          que supiera aconsejarse
          hoy en ocasión tan fuerte?
          ¿Habrá persona en el mundo
          a quien el cielo inclemente
          con más desdichas combata
          y con más pesares cerque?
          ¿Qué haré en tantas confusiones,
          donde imposible parece
          que halle razón que me alivie,
          ni alivio que me consuele?
          Desde la primer desdicha,
          no hay suceso ni accidente
          que otra desdicha no sea;
          que unas a otras suceden,

ROS.:   many a time.

ROS.:   I am your slave.

EST.:   Well, then, to tell it briefly,
my cousin Astolfo (let it suffice
for me to call him my cousin,
because there are some things that can be said
only in thoughts)
is to marry me,
if my fortune consents
to counterbalance so much bad luck
with one great piece of good luck.
I was grieved that, on the day we met,
he was wearing around his neck
the portrait of a lady;
I have spoken to him about it politely;
he's a gallant gentleman, and truly in love;
he's gone to fetch it, and he's supposed to bring it
here; I'm deeply embarrassed
by his coming to give it to me personally:
remain here, and, when he comes,
tell him to consign it
to you. I say no more;
you're clever and pretty,
and you must know what love is.   (*Exit.*)

ROS.:   How I wish I didn't know!
Heaven help me! Who could be
mindful enough and wise enough
to give herself good advice
in such a serious situation as this?
Can there be anyone in the world
whom unkind heaven
combats with more misfortunes
and besieges with more sorrows?
What should I do in such a dilemma,
in which it seems impossible
for me to find an idea to relieve me,
or relief to console me?
Ever since that first misfortune,
there hasn't been an event or an incident
that wasn't some new misfortune;
for they succeed one another

herederas de sí mismas.
A la imitación del Fénix,
unas de las otras nacen,
viviendo de lo que mueren,
y siempre de sus cenizas
está el sepulcro caliente.
Que eran cobardes, decía
un sabio, por parecerle
que nunca andaba una sola;
yo digo que son valientes,
pues siempre van adelante,
y nunca la espalda vuelven;
quien las llevare consigo,
a todo podrá atreverse,
pues en ninguna ocasión
no haya miedo que le dejen.
Dígalo yo, pues en tantas
como a mi vida suceden,
nunca me he hallado sin ellas,
ni se han cansado hasta verme
herida de la fortuna
en los brazos de la muerte.
¡Ay de mí! ¿qué debo hacer
hoy en la ocasión presente?
Si digo quién soy, Clotaldo,
a quien mi vida le debe
este amparo y este honor,
conmigo ofenderse puede,
pues me dice que callando
honor y remedio espere.
Si no he de decir quién soy
a Astolfo, y él llega a verme
¿cómo he de disimular?
Pues aunque fingirlo intenten
la voz, la lengua y los ojos,
les dirá el alma que mienten.
¿Qué haré? Mas ¿para qué estudio
lo que haré, si es evidente

as if each were the heir of the one before.
In emulation of the Phoenix,[19]
each one is born out of the preceding one,
living on its predecessor's death,
and the ashes of their grave
are always hot.
A philosopher once said
that misfortunes were cowards, because it seemed to him
that they never came singly;[20]
but I say that they're brave,
because they keep advancing,
and never turn their backs;
whoever has them for company
can undertake anything,
because there's no occasion
on which he can fear that they'll abandon him.
I'll vouch for it, since, on all the occasions
occurring in my life,
I've never found myself without them,
nor have they grown weary until seeing me
wounded by fortune
in the arms of death.
Woe is me! What am I to do
in the present situation?
If I reveal my identity, Clotaldo,
to whom my life owes
this protection and honor,
may be vexed with me,
since he has instructed me to be silent
while awaiting honor and redress.
If I don't reveal my identity
to Astolfo, but he gets to see me,
how can I dissemble?
Because, even if an attempt at pretense is made
by my voice, tongue, and eyes,
my soul will tell them that they're lying.
What shall I do? But why do I ponder
on what to do, if it's evident

---

19. The mythical bird reborn from its own ashes.   20. Compare: "When sorrows
come, they come not single spies, / But in battalions" (*Hamlet*, IV, v).

que por más que lo prevenga,
que lo estudie y que lo piense,
en llegando la ocasión
ha de hacer lo que quisiere
el dolor?, porque ninguno
imperio en sus penas tiene.
Y pues a determinar
lo que he de hacer no se atreve
el alma, llegue el dolor
hoy a su término, llegue
la pena a su extremo, y salga
de dudas y pareceres
de una vez; pero hasta entonces
¡valedme, cielos, valedme!

Sale ASTOLFO *con el retrato.*

AST.:   Este es, señora, el retrato;
         mas ¡ay Dios!
ROS.:   ¿Qué se suspende
         Vuestra Alteza? ¿qué se admira?
AST.:   De oírte, Rosaura, y verte.
ROS.:   ¿Yo Rosaura? Hase engañado
         Vuestra Alteza, ¿si me tiene
         por otra dama?; que yo
         soy Astrea, y no merece
         mi humildad tan grande dicha
         que esa turbación le cueste.
AST.:   Basta, Rosaura, el engaño,
         porque el alma nunca miente,
         y aunque como Astrea te mire,
         como a Rosaura te quiere.
ROS.:   No he entendido a Vuestra Alteza,
         y así no sé responderle.
         Sólo lo que yo diré
         es que Estrella (que lo puede
         ser de Venus) me mandó
         que en esta parte le espere,
         y de la suya le diga,
         que aquel retrato me entregue,
         que está muy puesto en razón,
         y yo misma se lo lleve.

that, no matter how I plan,
ponder, and plot,
when the moment comes
I will have to act under the dictates
of my sorrow? Because no one
has power over his own grief.
And, since my soul
isn't bold enough to decide
what I should do, let my sorrow reach
its limit today, let my pain
reach its extreme point, and let me energe
from my doubts and imaginings
once and for all. But, until that moment,
help me, heaven, help me!

Enter ASTOLFO *with the portrait.*

AST.:   My lady, here is the portrait;
        but—my God!
ROS.:   Why is Your Highness
        so dumbfounded? What surprises you?
AST.:   Hearing you, Rosaura, and seeing you.
ROS.:   I, Rosaura? Your Highness
        is deceived. Do you take me
        for some other lady? But I
        am Astraea, and my humble self
        doesn't deserve such great good fortune
        as to cause you such great confusion.
AST.:   Enough deception, Rosaura,
        because the soul never lies,
        and, though mine sees you as Astraea,
        it loves you as Rosaura.
ROS.:   I don't understand Your Highness,
        and so I don't know how to reply.
        The only thing I'll say
        is that Estrella (who is lovely enough
        to be the planet Venus) ordered me
        to wait for you here
        and tell you on her part
        to hand over that portrait to me,
        as is quite reasonable,
        so I myself can take it to her.

Estrella lo quiere así,
porque aun las cosas más leves
como sean en mi daño,
es Estrella quien las quiere.

AST.: Aunque más esfuerzos hagas,
¡oh qué mal, Rosaura, puedes
disimular! Di a los ojos
que su música concierten
con la voz; porque es forzoso
que desdiga y que disuene
tan destemplado instrumento,
que ajustar y medir quiere
la falsedad de quien dice,
con la verdad de quien siente.

ROS.: Ya digo que sólo espero
el retrato.

AST.:   Pues que quieres
llevar al fin el engaño,
con él quiero responderte.
Dirásle, Astrea, a la infanta,
que yo la estimo de suerte
que, pidiéndome un retrato,
poca fineza parece
enviársele, y así,
porque le estime y le precie
le envío el original;
y tú llevársele puedes,
pues ya le llevas contigo,
como a ti misma te lleves.

ROS.: Cuando un hombre se dispone,
restado, altivo y valiente,
a salir con una empresa,
aunque por trato le entreguen
lo que valga más, sin ella
necio y desairado vuelve.
Yo vengo por un retrato,
y aunque un original lleve
que vale más, volveré
desairada: y así, deme
Vuestra Alteza ese retrato,
que sin él no he de volverme.

That's what Estrella wants,
and even the slightest things,
though they may be to my detriment,
must be done when it's Estrella who wants them.

AST.: No matter what an effort you make,
Rosaura, oh, how badly you know how
to dissemble! Tell your eyes
to harmonize their music
with your voice; because of necessity
such an untuned instrument
will sound false and dissonant
when trying to adapt and regulate
the lies of the lips that speak
to the truth of the heart that feels.

ROS.: I tell you, I'm merely awaiting
the portrait.

AST.:   Since you wish
to carry the deception through to the end,
I shall answer you in the same terms.
Astraea, tell the princess
that I so esteem her
that, when she asks me for a portrait,
it seems to be lacking in politeness
merely to send it to her, and so,
because I esteem and value her,
I'm sending her the original;
and you are able to bring it to her
because you already have it with you
if you merely bring yourself.

ROS.: When a man is determined
daringly, proudly, and bravely
to accomplish an enterprise,
even if he is given in exchange
something worth more, without what he came for
he comes back home feeling foolish and awkward.
I have come for a portrait,
and even if I bring an original
that's worth more, I'll go back
feeling awkward; and so, give me
that portrait, Your Highness,
because I'm not going back without it.

AST.: ¿Pues cómo, si no he de darle,
le has de llevar?

ROS.: De esta suerte.
¡Suéltale, ingrato!

AST.: Es en vano.

ROS.: ¡Vive Dios, que no ha de verse
en manos de otra mujer!

AST.: Terrible estás.

ROS.: ¡Y tú aleve!

AST.: Ya basta, Rosaura mía.

ROS.: ¿Yo tuya, villano? Mientes.

Sale ESTRELLA.

EST.: Astrea, Astolfo, ¿qué es esto?

AST.: Aquésta es Estrella.

ROS.: Deme   (*Aparte.*)
para cobrar mi retrato,
ingenio el amor. Si quieres
saber lo que es, yo, señora,
te lo diré.

AST.: ¿Qué pretendes?

ROS.: Mandásteme que esperase
aquí a Astolfo, y le pidiese
un retrato de tu parte.
Quedé sola, y como vienen
de unos discursos a otros
las noticias fácilmente,
viéndote hablar de retratos,
con su memoria acordéme
de que tenía uno mío
en la manga, quise verle,
porque una persona sola
con locuras se divierte.
Cayóseme de la mano
al suelo; Astolfo, que viene
a entregarte el de otra dama,
le levantó, y tan rebelde
está en dar el que le pides,
que en vez de dar uno, quiere
llevar otro. Pues el mío
aún no es posible volverme

AST.:   And if I don't give it to you, how
         will you manage to bring it?
ROS.:   This way!
         Let go of it, faithless man!
AST.:   It's useless.
ROS.:   As God lives, it will never be seen
         in another woman's hands!
AST.:   You're a terror!
ROS.:   And you're a deceiver!
AST.:   Enough now, Rosaura dear.
ROS.:   Dear to you, lowlife? You're lying!

                     Enter ESTRELLA.

EST.:   Astraea, Astolfo, what's going on?
AST.:   Estrella is here.
ROS.:   (*Aside:*) May love
         provide me with a ruse to recover
         my portrait! My lady,
         if you wish to know what's happening, I
         will tell you.
AST.:   What do you have in mind?
ROS.:   You ordered me to wait
         for Astolfo here and ask him for
         a portrait that you wanted.
         I remained alone, and since thoughts
         move easily
         from one topic to another,
         when I heard you speak of portraits,
         that mention made me recall
         that I had one of myself
         in my sleeve; I took a notion to look at it,
         because a person left all alone
         amuses himself with silly things.
         It fell out of my hand
         onto the floor; Astolfo, who was coming
         to hand over to you that of another lady,
         picked it up, and was so reluctant
         to give the one you asked him for
         that, instead of giving one, he wanted
         to take two. Since it still
         hasn't been possible to get my own back

  con ruegos y persuasiones,
  colérica y impaciente
  yo se le quise quitar.
  Aquel que en la mano tiene
  es mío; tú lo verás
  con ver si se me parece.

EST.: Soltad, Astolfo, el retrato.   (*Quítasele.*)

AST.: Señora . . .

EST.:   No son crueles
  a la verdad los matices.

ROS.: ¿No es mío?

EST.:   ¿Qué duda tiene?

ROS.: Di que ahora te entregue el otro.

EST.: Toma tu retrato, y vete.

ROS.: Yo he cobrado mi retrato,
  venga ahora lo que viniere.   (*Vase.*)

EST.: Dadme ahora el retrato vos
  que os pedí, que aunque no piense
  veros ni hablaros jamás,
  no quiero, no, que se quede
  en vuestro poder, siquiera
  porque yo tan neciamente
  le he pedido.

AST.:   ¿Cómo puedo   (*Aparte.*)
  salir de lance tan fuerte?
  Aunque quiera, hermosa Estrella,
  servirte y obedecerte,
  no podré darte el retrato
  que me pides, porque . . .

EST.:   Eres
  villano y grosero amante.
  No quiero que me le entregues;
  porque yo tampoco quiero,
  con tomarle, que me acuerdes
  de que yo te le he pedido.   (*Vase.*)

AST.: ¡Oye, escucha, mira, advierte!
  ¡Válgate Dios por Rosaura!
  ¿Dónde, cómo o de qué suerte
  hoy a Polonia has venido
  a perderme y a perderte?

through entreaty or persuasion,
I became angry and impatient,
and tried to take it away from him.
The one he's holding in his hand
is mine; you'll be convinced of that
if you look and see the resemblance to me.

EST.: Astolfo, let go of the portrait!   (*She takes it from him.*)

AST.: My lady . . .

EST.:   Indeed,
the painted likeness isn't unfaithful to life.

ROS.: Isn't it a picture of me?

EST.:   How can anyone doubt it?

ROS.: Tell him to hand the other one over to you now.

EST.: Take your own portrait and go!

ROS.: I've recovered my portrait;
now: come what may!   (*Exit.*)

EST.: Now give me the portrait
I asked you for, because, even though I don't intend
ever to see you or speak to you again,
I don't want it to remain
in your possession, if only
because I so foolishly
asked you for it.

AST.:   (*Aside:*) How can I
get out of such an awful situation?
Beautiful Estrella, even though I wish
to serve you and obey you,
I can't give you the portrait
you ask for, because . . .

EST.:   You're
a low, coarse suitor!
I don't want you to hand it over to me;
because I don't want
you to remind me (if I take it)
that I asked you for it.   (*Exit.*)

AST.: Hear me, listen, look, let me explain!
Damn you, Rosaura!
From where, how, in what way
did you come to Poland today
to ruin me and ruin yourself?

Descúbrese SEGISMUNDO *como al principio,*
con pieles y cadena, durmiendo en el suelo.
Salen CLOTALDO, CLARÍN *y los dos criados.*

CLO.:   Aquí le habéis de dejar,
          pues hoy su soberbia acaba
          donde empezó.

CRI. 1.°:   Como estaba
          la cadena vuelvo a atar.

CLA.:   No acabes de despertar,
          Segismundo, para verte
          perder, trocada la suerte,
          siendo tu gloria fingida,
          una sombra de la vida
          y una llama de la muerte.

CLO.:   A quien sabe discurrir
          así, es bien que se prevenga
          una estancia, donde tenga
          harto lugar de argüir.
          Este es el que habéis de asir,
          y en ese cuarto encerrar.

CLA.:   ¿Por qué a mí?

CLO.:   Porque ha de estar
          guardado en prisión tan grave,
          Clarín que secretos sabe,
          donde no pueda sonar.

CLA.:   ¿Yo, por dicha, solicito
          dar muerte a mi padre? No.
          ¿Arrojé del balcón yo
          al Icaro de poquito?
          ¿Yo muero ni resucito?
          ¿Yo sueño o duermo? ¿A qué fin
          me encierran?

CLO.:   Eres Clarín.

CLA.:   Pues ya digo que seré
          corneta, y que callaré,
          que es instrumento ruin.   (*Llévanle.*)

Sale el REY BASILIO *rebozado.*

SEGISMUNDO *is discovered as at the beginning of the play,*
dressed in skins and chained, asleep on the ground.
Enter CLOTALDO, CLARÍN, *and two* SERVANTS.

CLO.: You are to leave him here,
since today his pridefulness ends
where it began.

SER. 1:   I am reattaching
the chain the way it was.

CLA.: Don't wake up,
Segismundo, to see your
downfall, your change of fate,
because your glory was a pretense,
a shadow of life
and a will-o'-the-wisp.[21]

CLO.: A man wise enough to utter
such a discourse ought to be provided
with a lodging where he'll have
plenty of time to philosophize.
Seize this man
and lock him in that room!

CLA.: Why are you doing this to *me?*

CLO.:   Because one must
guard in a prison as secure as this
a "Clarion" who knows secrets,
so he won't blare and blurt them out.

CLA.: Is it I, by chance, who am trying
to kill my father? No.
Did *I* throw from the balcony
that low-scale Icarus?[22]
Do I die or come back to life?
Do I dream or sleep? To what purpose
am I being locked up?

CLO.:   You're a "Clarion."

CLA.: In that case, I promise to be
a bugle, and to keep quiet,
because that's a vulgar instrument!   (*They take him out.*)

Enter King BASILIO, *muffed in his cloak.*

---

21. Some editors read *una imagen de la muerte* ("an image of death").   22. The son of Daedalus who fell into the sea during their escape from Crete when the wax that held his artificial wings to his body melted in the sun's heat.

BAS.:   Clotaldo.

CLO.:   ¡Señor! ¿así
          viene Vuestra Majestad?

BAS.:   La necia curiosidad
          de ver lo que pasa aquí
          a Segismundo (¡ay de mí!)
          de este modo me ha traído.

CLO.:   Mírale allí reducido
          a su miserable estado.

BAS.:   ¡Ay, príncipe desdichado,
          y en triste punto nacido!
             Llega a despertarle ya,
          que fuerza y vigor perdió
          ese lotos que bebió.

CLO.:   Inquieto, señor, está,
          y hablando.

BAS.:   ¿Qué soñará
          ahora? Escuchemos, pues.

SEG.:   Piadoso príncipe es   (*En sueños.*)
          el que castiga tiranos,
          muera Clotaldo a mis manos,
          bese mi padre mis pies.

CLO.:   Con la muerte me amenaza.

BAS.:   A mí con rigor y afrenta.

CLO.:   Quitarme la vida intenta.

BAS.:   Rendirme a sus plantas traza.

SEG.:   Salga a la anchurosa plaza   (*En sueños.*)
          del gran teatro del mundo
          este valor sin segundo,
          porque mi venganza cuadre.
          Vean triunfar de su padre
          al príncipe Segismundo.
             Mas ¡ay de mí! ¿dónde estoy?   (*Despierta.*)

BAS.:   Pues a mí no me ha de ver.
          Ya sabes lo que has de hacer,
          desde allí a escucharte voy.   (*Retírase.*)

SEG.:   ¿Soy yo por ventura? ¿Soy
          el que preso y aherrojado
          llego a verme en tal estado?

BAS.:   Clotaldo!
CLO.:   Sire! Is this the way
          for Your Majesty to appear?
BAS.:   My foolish curiosity
          to see what's happening here
          to Segismundo (woe is me!)
          brings me here in this fashion.
CLO.:   Behold him there brought back down
          to his lowly condition.
BAS.:   Alas, unfortunate prince,
          born at an unhappy hour!
               Go over and awaken him now,
          because that narcotic he drank
          has lost its strength and power.
CLO.:   He's restless, Sire,
          and he's saying something.
BAS.:   What can he be dreaming of
          now? Let's listen.
SEG.:   (dreaming): A prince is only being merciful
          when he punishes tyrants;
          let Clotaldo die at my hands,
          let my father kiss my feet!
CLO.:   He threatens me with death.
BAS.:   And me with severity and insult.
CLO.:   He plans to take my life.
BAS.:   He intends to make me fall at his feet.
SEG: (dreaming): Let my matchless worth
          sally forth onto the spacious grounds
          of the great theater of the world,[23]
          so that my revenge may be adequate!
          Let everyone see Prince
          Segismundo triumphing over his father!
               (Awakening) But, woe is me! Where am I?
BAS.:   He mustn't see me.
          You know what you must do;
          I'm going over there, where I can listen to you. (He withdraws.)
SEG.:   Is this perchance me? Am I
          the one, a captive in irons,
          finding myself in this condition?

23. The title of a Calderón play (see Introduction).

          ¿No sois mi sepulcro vos,
          torre? Sí. ¡Válgame Dios,
          qué de cosas he soñado!

CLO.:   A mí me toca llegar
          a hacer la deshecha ahora.—
          ¿Es ya de despertar hora?

SEG.:   Sí, hora es ya de despertar.

CLO.:   ¿Todo el día te has de estar
          durmiendo? ¿Desde que yo
          al águila que voló
          con tarda vista seguí,
          y te quedaste tú aquí,
          nunca has despertado?

SEG.:   No,
          ni aun ahora he despertado,
          que según, Clotaldo, entiendo,
          todavía estoy durmiendo.
          Y no estoy muy engañado;
          porque si ha sido soñado,
          lo que vi palpable y cierto,
          lo que veo será incierto;
          y no es mucho que rendido,
          pues veo estando dormido,
          que sueñe estando despierto.

CLO.:   Lo que soñaste me di.

SEG.:   Supuesto que sueño fue,
          no diré lo que soñé,
          lo que vi, Clotaldo, sí.
          Yo desperté y yo me vi
          (¡qué crueldad tan lisonjera!)
          en un lecho que pudiera,
          con matices y colores,
          ser el catre de las flores
          que tejió la Primavera.
          Allí mil nobles, rendidos
          a mis pies, nombre me dieron
          de su príncipe, y sirvieron
          galas, joyas y vestidos.

             Aren't you my tomb,
             tower? Yes. God help me,
             all the things I dreamt!
CLO.:   It's my duty to go
             and disillusion him now.—
             Is it already time to get up?
SEG.:   Yes, it's already time to get up.
CLO.:   Must you spend the whole day
             sleeping? From the time when I
             followed that flying eagle
             with my laggard sight,[24]
             and you remained here,
             you've never awakened?
SEG.:   No,
                 nor have I awakened even now,
             Clotaldo, because, as far as I can tell,
             I'm still asleep.
             And I'm not far wrong;
             because if what I saw palpably and surely
             was just a dream,
             what I see now is probably doubtful;
             and it wouldn't be a surprise that,
             if I see clearly while asleep,
             I should dream while awake.
CLO.:   Tell me what you dreamt.
SEG.:   Since it was a dream,
             I won't say what I "dreamt,"
             Clotaldo, but what I "saw."
             I awoke and found myself
             (what flattering cruelty!)
             in a bed that,
             with its tints and colors,
             might have been the flowery cot
             woven by the springtime.
                 There a thousand noblemen, submissive
             to me, called me
             their prince, and offered me
             finery, jewels, and clothes.

---

24. Some editors read *con tardo vuelo* ("with [the] laggard flight [of my own eyes]";
or: "with sluggish faculties").

La calma de mis sentidos
tú trocaste en alegría,
diciendo la dicha mía;
que aunque estoy de esta manera,
príncipe en Polonia era.
CLO.: Buenas albricias tendría.
SEG.: No muy buenas: por traidor,
con pecho atrevido y fuerte
dos veces te daba muerte.
CLO.: ¿Para mí tanto rigor?
SEG.: De todos era señor,
y de todos me vengaba;
sólo a una mujer amaba;
que fue verdad, creo yo,
en que todo se acabó,
y esto sólo no se acaba. (*Vase el rey.*)
CLO.: Enternecido se ha ido
el rey de haberle escuchado.
Como habíamos hablado
de aquella águila, dormido,
tu sueño imperios han sido,
mas en sueños fuera bien
entonces, honrar a quien
te crió en tantos empeños,
Segismundo, que aun en sueños
no se pierde el hacer bien. (*Vase.*)
SEG.: Es verdad, pues: reprimamos
esta fiera condición,
esta furia, esta ambición,
por si alguna vez soñamos.
Y sí haremos, pues estamos
en mundo tan singular,
que el vivir sólo es soñar;
y la experiencia me enseña,
que el hombre que vive, sueña
lo que es, hasta despertar.
Sueña el rey que es rey, y vive
con este engaño mandando,
disponiendo y gobernando;
y este aplauso, que recibe
prestado, en el viento escribe

You yourself changed the numbness
of my senses into joy
when you told me of my good fortune;
because, even though I am here like this,
I was the prince of Poland.
CLO.:   You must have given me a good reward for the news.
SEG.:   Not very good: calling you traitor,
with a rash, strong heart
I tried twice to kill you.
CLO.:   So harsh with me?
SEG.:   I was lord over all,
and was taking revenge on all;
I loved one woman alone;
I believe that that really happened,
because everything else has vanished,
but that love alone stays with me.   (*Exit King* BASILIO.)
CLO.:   The king has departed,
touched by what he heard him say.
Since we had been speaking
about that eagle, when you slept
you dreamt of empire,
but even in dreams it would have been proper
at that time to honor the man
who raised you with such great pains,
Segismundo, because even in dreams
good deeds are never wasted.   (*Exit.*)
SEG.:   It's true, then: let me restrain
my fierce nature,
my fury, my ambition,
in case I ever dream again.
And I *will*, since we exist
in such a peculiar world
that living is merely dreaming;
and the experience teaches me
that the man who lives dreams
his reality until he awakes.
    The king dreams that he's king, and lives
in that deception, giving orders,
making decisions, and ruling;
and that acclaim, which he receives
as a loan, is written on the wind

en cenizas le convierte
la muerte (¡desdicha fuerte!):
¡que hay quien intente reinar
viendo que ha de despertar
en el sueño de la muerte!
    Sueña el rico en su riqueza,
que más cuidados le ofrece;
sueña el pobre que padece
su miseria y su pobreza;
sueña el que a medrar empieza,
sueña el que afana y pretende,
sueña el que agravia y ofende,
y en el mundo, en conclusión,
todos sueñan lo que son,
aunque ninguno lo entiende.
    Yo sueño que estoy aquí,
de estas prisiones cargado;
y soñé que en otro estado
más lisonjero me vi.
¿Qué es la vida? Un frenesí.
¿Qué es la vida? Una ilusión,
una sombra, una ficción,
y el mayor bien es pequeño;
que toda la vida es sueño,
y los sueños, sueños son.

and changed into ashes
by death (a great misfortune!):
to think that there are people who try to reign
knowing that they must awaken
in the sleep of death!
     The rich man dreams about his riches,
which cause him greater worries;
the poor man dreams that he is suffering
his misery and poverty;
the man beginning to thrive is just dreaming,
the man who toils and strives is just dreaming,
the man who affronts and injures is just dreaming;
and, to sum up, in this world
all men merely dream what they are,
though no one realizes it.
     I'm dreaming that I'm here,
laden with these shackles;
and I dreamt that I found myself
in another, more flattering condition.
What is life? A frenzy.
What is life? An illusion,
a shadow, a fiction,
and our greatest good is but small;
for, all of life is a dream,
and even dreams are dreams.

Jornada tercera

Sale CLARÍN.

CLA.:   En una encantada torre,
por lo que sé, vivo preso.
¿Qué me harán por lo que ignoro,
si por lo que sé me han muerto?
¿Que un hombre con tanta hambre
viniese a morir viviendo?
Lástima tengo de mí;
todos dirán: «Bien lo creo»;
y bien se puede creer,
pues para mí este silencio
no conforma con el nombre
Clarín, y callar no puedo.
Quien me hace compañía
aquí (si a decirlo acierto),
son arañas y ratones,
¡miren qué dulces jilgueros!
De los sueños de esta noche
la triste cabeza tengo
llena de mil chirimías,
de trompetas y embelecos,
de procesiones, de cruces,
de disciplinantes; y éstos,
unos suben, otros bajan;
otros se desmayan viendo
la sangre que llevan otros;
mas yo, la verdad diciendo,
de no comer me desmayo;
que en una prisión me veo,

Act Three

Enter CLARÍN.

CLA.:   In an enchanted tower
I live a captive, because of what I know.
What will they do to me for what I *don't* know,
if they've killed me for what I do know?
To think that a man with a hunger like mine[25]
should have such a living death!
I feel sorry for myself;
everybody will say, "I readily believe it";
and it *can* be readily believed,
because, to me, this silence
doesn't suit the name
"Clarion," and I'm unable to remain silent.
The only ones keeping me company
here (if I'm correct in saying it)
are spiders and mice—
just see, what sweet-voiced goldfinches!
After my dreams from last night
I have my sad head
filled with a thousand shawms,
trumpets, and delusions,
processions, crosses,
and flagellants; and some
of them march upward, others downward;
some of them faint away when they see
the blood streaming from others;
but I, to tell the truth,
am fainting away from not eating;
because I find myself in a prison

---

25. The wordplay on *hombre* and *hambre* can't be matched in English.

donde ya todos los días
en el filósofo leo
Nicomedes, y las noches
en el concilio Niceno.
Si llaman santo al callar,
como en calendario nuevo,
San Secreto es para mí,
pues le ayuno y no le huelgo;
aunque está bien merecido
el castigo que padezco,
pues callé, siendo criado,
que es el mayor sacrilegio.

Ruido de cajas y gente, y dicen [SOLDADOS] *dentro.*

SOL. 1.°: Esta es la torre en que está.
Echad la puerta en el suelo.
Entrad todos.
CLA.:   ¡Vive Dios
que a mí me buscan! Es cierto,
pues que dicen que aquí estoy.
¿Qué me querrán?

Salen los SOLDADOS *que pudieren.*

SOL. 1.°:   Entrad dentro.
SOL. 2.°: Aquí está.
CLA.:   No está.
TODOS: Señor . . .
CLA.:   ¿Si vienen borrachos éstos?
SOL. 2.°: Tú nuestro príncipe eres;
ni admitimos ni queremos
sino al señor natural,
y no príncipe extranjero.
A todos nos da los pies.
TODOS: ¡Viva el gran príncipe nuestro!
CLA.:   Vive Dios, que va de veras.
¿Si es costumbre en este reino
prender uno cada día

in which every day
I read the philosopher
Nicomedes, and every night
I read about the Nicene Council.[26]
If they call being silent saintly,
as if in a new religious calendar,[27]
then my patron is Saint Secret,[28]
since I fast in his honor, but don't have a banquet;
and yet, the punishment
I'm suffering is well deserved,
because, servant that I am, I kept quiet,
and that's the greatest sacrilege!

Noise of drums and people; voices [of SOLDIERS] *from within.*

SOL. 1: This is the tower in which he's kept.
Knock the door down to the ground!
Everyone enter!

CLA.:   As God lives,
they're looking for *me!* It must be,
because they're saying I'm kept here.
What can they want of me?

Enter as many SOLDIERS *as possible.*

SOL. 1:   Come in here!
SOL. 2: Here he is!
CLA.:   No, he's not.
ALL: Sire . . .
CLA.: Can they be drunk?
SOL. 2: You are our prince;
we don't accept or want anyone
but our natural lord,
and not a foreign prince.
Give all of us your feet to kiss!
ALL: Long live our great prince!
CLA.: As God lives, they're serious!
Is it a custom in this kingdom
to arrest someone every day

---

26. Untranslatable puns in Spanish: *Nicomedes* suggests *ni como* ("and I don't eat"), while *Niceno* can be thought of as *ni ceno* ("and I don't sup").   27. Just possibly a reference to the Gregorian calendar, introduced in 1582.   28. An imaginary, proverbial saint.

y hacerle príncipe, y luego
volverle a la torre? Sí,
pues cada día lo veo:
fuerza es hacer mi papel.

TODOS: Danos tus plantas.

CLA.:   No puedo
porque las he menester
para mí, y fuera defeto
ser príncipe desplantado.

SOL. 2.°: Todos a tu padre mesmo
le dijimos, que a ti sólo
por príncipe conocemos,
no al de Moscovia.

CLA.:   ¿A mi padre
le perdisteis el respeto?
Sois unos tales por cuales.

SOL. 1.°: Fue lealtad de nuestros pechos.

CLA.: Si fue lealtad, yo os perdono.

SOL. 2.°: Sal a restaurar tu imperio.
¡Viva Segismundo!

TODOS: ¡Viva!

CLA.: Segismundo dicen, ¡bueno!
Segismundos llaman todos
los príncipes contrahechos.

Sale SEGISMUNDO.

SEG.: ¿Quién nombra aquí a Segismundo?

CLA.: ¿Mas que soy príncipe huero?

SOL. 2.°: ¿Quién es Segismundo?

SEG.:   Yo.

SOL. 2.°: ¿Pues cómo, atrevido y necio,
tú te hacías Segismundo?

CLA.: ¿Yo Segismundo? Eso niego.
Vosotros fuisteis los que
me segismundasteis: luego
vuestra ha sido solamente
necedad y atrevimiento.

SOL. 1.°: Gran príncipe Segismundo,

and make him prince, and then
send him back to the tower? Yes,
because I see it happening daily:
I've got to play my part.

ALL: Give us your soles!

CLA.:   I can't,
because I need them
for myself, and it would be a defect
to be a soulless prince.[29]

SOL. 2: We have all told your father
himself that we recognize
you alone as prince,
not the man from Muscovy.

CLA.:   You've lost
your respect for my father?
You're a bunch of no-goods!

SOL. 1: It was the loyalty of our hearts.

CLA.:   If it was loyalty, I forgive you.

SOL. 2: Come out and recover your sovereignty.
Long live Segismundo!

ALL: Long may he live!

CLA.:   They're saying "Segismundo"—all right!
They must give the name Segismundo
to every fake prince.

Enter SEGISMUNDO.

SEG.:   Who is mentioning Segismundo's name here?

CLA.:   Does this mean I'm a rotten egg of a prince?

SOL. 2: Which one is Segismundo?

SEG.:   I am.

SOL. 2: Then why, you insolent fool,
were you pretending to be Segismundo?

CLA.:   I, Segismundo? I deny it.
It was you who
segismundized me; and so,
you were the only ones who were
foolish and insolent.

SOL. 1: Great Prince Segismundo

29. In the Spanish original, the pun is different: the soldiers ask for the prince's *plantas* ("soles" = "feet"), and Clarín replies that, if he gave them away, he'd be *desplantado* ("uprooted," literally "unplanted").

(que las señas que traemos
tuyas son, aunque por fe
te aclamamos señor nuestro).
Tu padre, el gran rey Basilio,
temeroso que los cielos
cumplan un hado, que dice
que ha de verse a tus pies puesto
vencido de ti, pretende
quitarte acción y derecho
y dársela a Astolfo, duque
de Moscovia. Para esto
juntó su corte, y el vulgo,
penetrando ya y sabiendo
que tiene rey natural,
no quiere que un extranjero
venga a mandarle. Y así,
haciendo noble desprecio
de la inclemencia del hado,
te ha buscado donde preso
vives, para que valido
de sus armas, y saliendo
de esta torre a restaurar
tu imperial corona y cetro,
se la quites a un tirano.
Sal, pues; que en ese desierto,
ejército numeroso
de bandidos y plebeyos
te aclama: la libertad
te espera: oye sus acentos.

VOCES: ¡Viva Segismundo, viva!   (*Dentro.*)
SEG.:   Otra vez (¿qué es esto, cielos?),
         ¿queréis que sueñe grandezas,
         que ha de deshacer el tiempo?
         ¿Otra vez queréis que vea
         entre sombras y bosquejos
         la majestad y la pompa
         desvanecida del viento?
         ¿Otra vez queréis que toque
         el desengaño, o el riesgo

(for, the description we have
matches you, although we acclaim you
as our lord on faith):
Your father, great King Basilio,
fearing that heaven
would fulfill a prophecy that said
he would find himself stretched at your feet,
conquered by you, is planning
to deprive you of your freedom of action and your rights
and to give them to Astolfo, duke
of Muscovy. For that purpose
he assembled his court, but the commoners,
now learning and knowing
that they have a natural successor,
refuse to let a foreigner
come and command them. And so,
nobly scorning
the harshness of the prophecy,
they have searched you out where you dwell
as a prisoner, in order that, assisted
by their weapons, you may leave
this tower and recover
your imperial crown and scepter,
taking them away from a tyrant.
Then, do come out; for, in this wilderness,
a numerous army
of outlaws[30] and plebeians
acclaims you: liberty
awaits you: listen to its voice!

VOICES (*within*): Long live Segismundo! Long may he live!
SEG.:   Once again (what can this be, heavens?)
you want me to dream of grandeur
which time must undo?
Once again you want me to see,
amid shadows and sketchy forms,
majesty and pomp
dispersed by the wind?
Once again you want me to experience
disillusionment, or the risk

---

30. It has been suggested that here *bandidos* refers merely to lower-class people.

a que el humano poder
nace humilde y vive atento?
Pues no ha de ser, no ha de ser;
miradme otra vez sujeto
a mi fortuna; y pues sé
que toda esta vida es sueño,
idos, sombras, que fingís
hoy a mis sentidos muertos
cuerpo y voz, siendo verdad
que ni tenéis voz ni cuerpo;
que no quiero majestades
fingidas, pompas no quiero
fantásticas, ilusiones
que al soplo menos ligero
del aura han de deshacerse,
bien como el florido almendro,
que por madrugar sus flores,
sin aviso y sin consejo,
al primer soplo se apagan,
marchitando y desluciendo
de sus rosados capillos
belleza, luz y ornamento.
Ya os conozco, ya os conozco,
y sé que os pasa lo mesmo
con cualquiera que se duerme.
Para mí no hay fingimientos,
que, desengañado ya,
sé bien que *la vida es sueño*.

SOL. 2.°: Si piensas que te engañamos,
vuelve a esos montes soberbios
los ojos, para que veas
la gente que aguarda en ellos
para obedecerte.

SEG.:   Ya
otra vez vi aquesto mesmo
tan clara y distintamente
como ahora lo estoy viendo,
y fue sueño.

SOL. 2.°:   Cosas grandes
siempre, gran señor, trajeron
anuncios; y esto sería,

into which human power
is humbly born, and of which it is constantly made aware?
Well, it won't happen, it won't happen;
behold me once again subject
to my fortune; and, since I know
that all of this life is a dream,
away with you, you shadows that today
pretend to my numbed senses
that you have a body and a voice, though the truth is
you have neither voice nor body;
for I don't want majesty
that is feigned, I don't want pomp
that is imaginary, illusions
that at the slightest puff
of the breeze will disintegrate,
exactly like a blossoming almond tree,
which because its blooms appeared too early,
unadvisedly and imprudently,
finds them extinguished by the first gust,
withering and losing
the beauty, light, and adornment
of their pink buds.
I know you by now, I know you by now,
and I know that you do the same thing
to everyone who falls asleep.
For me there is no more pretense,
because, now undeceived,
I know perfectly well that LIFE IS A DREAM.
SOL. 2: If you think we're fooling you,
turn your eyes to those
arrogant mountains, so you can see
the soldiers waiting there
to obey your orders.
SEG.:   Once before
in the past I saw the very same thing
just as clearly and distinctly
as I see it now,
and it was a dream.
SOL. 2:   Great lord,
great events have always induced
presentiments; and that must now be the case,

si lo soñaste primero.

SEG.: Dices bien, anuncio fue,
y caso que fuese cierto,
pues que la vida es tan corta,
soñemos, alma, soñemos
otra vez; pero ha de ser
con atención y consejo
de que hemos de despertar
de este gusto al mejor tiempo;
que llevándolo sabido,
será el desengaño menos;
que es hacer burla del daño
adelantarle el consejo.
Y con esta prevención
de que cuando fuese cierto,
es todo el poder prestado
y ha de volverse a su dueño,
atrevámonos a todo.
Vasallos, yo os agradezco
la lealtad; en mí lleváis
quien os libre osado y diestro
de extranjera esclavitud.
Tocad al arma, que presto
veréis mi inmenso valor.
Contra mi padre pretendo
tomar armas, y sacar
verdaderos a los cielos.
Presto he de verle a mis plantas.
Mas si antes de esto despierto,
¿no será bien no decirlo,
supuesto que no he de hacerlo?

TODOS: ¡Viva Segismundo, viva!

Sale CLOTALDO.

CLO.: ¿Qué alboroto es éste, cielos?

SEG.: Clotaldo.

CLO.:   Señor. (*Aparte.*) En mí
su crueldad prueba.

CLA.:   Yo apuesto
que le despeña del monte.   (*Vase.*)

CLO.: A tus reales plantas llego,

if you dreamed it earlier.

SEG.: You're right, it was a presentiment,
and in case it was accurate,
seeing that life is so short,
let us dream, my soul, let us dream
once again; but now it must be
with the awareness and knowledge
that we must awaken
from this pleasurable dream just when we're happiest;
for, keeping that in mind,
our disappointment won't be so great;
because to take counsel against harm
in advance is to laugh at it.
And with this foreknowledge
that, even if the presentiment should be true,
all my power is merely borrowed
and must return to its Owner,
let us adventure everything!
Vassals, I thank you
for your loyalty; in me you have
a man who will boldly and skillfully free you
from foreign servitude.
Sound the alarm, for swiftly
you shall see my boundless valor!
I intend to take arms
against my father, and make
heaven's prediction come true.
I shall soon see him at my feet.
But, if I awaken before that,
won't it be better not to mention it,
because I won't actually do it?

ALL: Long live Segismundo! Long may he live!

Enter CLOTALDO.

CLO.: Heavens, what is this hubbub?
SEG.: Clotaldo!
CLO.:   Sire? (*Aside:*) He wants
to try out his cruelty on me.
CLA.:   I bet
he'll throw him off the mountain!   (*Exit.*)
CLO.: I fall at your royal feet,

ya sé que a morir.

SEG.:   Levanta,
levanta, padre, del suelo;
que tú has de ser norte y guía
de quien fíe mis aciertos;
que ya sé que mi crianza
a tu mucha lealtad debo.
Dame los brazos.

CLO.:   ¿Qué dices?

SEG.:   Que estoy soñando, y que quiero
obrar bien, pues no se pierde
obrar bien, aun entre sueños.

CLO.:   Pues, señor, si el obrar bien
es ya tu blasón, es cierto
que no te ofenda el que yo
hoy solicite lo mesmo.
¿A tu padre has de hacer guerra?
Yo aconsejarte no puedo
contra mi rey, ni valerte.
A tus plantas estoy puesto,
dame la muerte.

SEG.:   ¡Villano,
traidor, ingrato! Mas ¡cielos!
reportarme me conviene,
que aún no sé si estoy despierto.
Clotaldo, vuestro valor
os envidio y agradezco.
Idos a servir al rey,
que en el campo nos veremos.—
Vosotros tocad al arma.

CLO.:   Mil veces tus plantas beso.

SEG.:   A reinar, fortuna, vamos;
no me despiertes si duermo,
y si es verdad, no me duermas.
Mas sea verdad o sueño,
obrar bien es lo que importa;
si fuere verdad, por serlo;
si no, por ganar amigos
para cuando despertemos.

Vanse y tocan al arma. Salen el REY BASILIO *y* ASTOLFO.

SEG.:   though I know it means my death.

SEG.:   Rise,
        rise, father, from the ground;
        for you must be the North Star and guide
        to whom I entrust my success;
        for I now know that I owe
        my upbringing to your great loyalty.
        Come and embrace me.

CLO.:   What are you saying?

SEG.:   That I'm dreaming, and that I wish
        to do good, because good deeds
        aren't wasted, even in dreams.

CLO.:   Well, Sire, if doing good
        is now your motto, I'm sure
        you won't be offended if I
        have the same goal today.
        Should you make war on your father?
        I cannot be your counselor,
        or help you, against my king.
        I am prostrate at your feet,
        kill me.

SEG.:   Base,
        disloyal traitor! But, heavens,
        it behooves me to calm down,
        because I don't yet know whether I'm awake.
        Clotaldo, I envy you
        and thank you for your great worth.
        Go and serve the king,
        for we shall meet on the field of battle.—
        You there, sound the alarm!

CLO.:   I kiss your feet a thousand times.

SEG.:   Fortune, let me go and reign!
        Don't awaken me if I'm asleep,
        and, if this is reality, don't put me to sleep.
        But, whether it's reality or a dream,
        to do good is what matters;
        if it should be reality, just because it *is* good;
        if not, for the sake of winning friends
        for the time when we awaken.

They exit, sounding the alarm. Enter King BASILIO *and* ASTOLFO.

BAS.:   ¿Quién, Astolfo, podrá para prudente
la furia de un caballo desbocado?
¿Quién detener de un río la corriente
que corre al mar soberbio y despeñado?
¿Quién un peñasco suspender valiente
de la cima de un monte desgajado?
Pues todo fácil de parar ha sido
y un vulgo no, soberbio y atrevido.
Dígalo en bandos el rumor partido,
pues se oye resonar en lo profundo
de los montes el eco repetido,
unos *¡Astolfo!* y otros *¡Segismundo!*
El dosel de la jura, reducido
a segunda intención, a horror segundo,
teatro funesto es, donde importuna
representa tragedia la fortuna.

AST.:   Suspéndase, señor, el alegría,
cese el aplauso y gusto lisonjero,
que tu mano feliz me prometía;
que si Polonia (a quien mandar espero)
hoy se resiste a la obediencia mía,
es porque la merezca yo primero.
Dadme un caballo y de arrogancia lleno,
rayo descienda el que blasona trueno.

                                   (Vase.)

BAS.:   Poco reparo tiene lo infalible,
y mucho riesgo lo previsto tiene:
si ha de ser, la defensa es imposible,
que quien la excusa más, más la previene.

¡Dura ley! ¡fuerte caso! ¡horror terrible!
Quien piensa que huye el riesgo, al riesgo viene;
con lo que yo guardaba me he perdido;
yo mismo, yo mi patria he destruido.

              Sale ESTRELLA.

EST.:   Si tu presencia, gran señor, no trata
de enfrenar el tumulto sucedido,
que de uno en otro bando se dilata,
por las calles y plazas dividido,
verás tu reino en ondas de escarlata

BAS.:   Who, Astolfo, can prudently check
          the fury of a runaway horse?
          Who can hold back the current of a river
          that flows toward the sea proudly and precipitously?
          Who can bravely halt the course of a boulder
          detached from the summit of a mountain?
          Well, all of those are easy to stop,
          but not an entire nation in its pridefulness and daring.
          The shouts of the divided factions will vouch for that,
          since one hears resounding in the depths
          of the mountains their repeated echo,
          some crying "Astolfo!" and others, "Segismundo!"
          The throne of law, perverted into something
          it was never meant to be, into a scene of horror,
          is a grisly theater, where wanton
          Fortune stages tragedies.

AST.:   Sire, call a halt to the wedding merriment,
          put an end to the acclaim and the flattering pleasures
          which your felicitous hand promised me;
          for, if Poland (which I hope to rule)
          is resisting against allegiance to me today,
          it's because I must first earn it.
          Give me a horse, and, filled with boldness,
          let the man who is boasting like thunder descend like lightning!
                                                              (*Exit.*)

BAS.:   What is infallible can't very well be averted,
          and there is great risk in what is foreknown:
          if it must come about, defense is impossible,
          because the man who tries hardest to avoid it, prepares it more
               readily.
          Harsh law! Cruel event! Terrible horror!
          The man who thinks he's fleeing danger runs into it;
          by keeping things hidden, I ruined myself;
          I, I myself, have destroyed my country!

                         Enter ESTRELLA.

EST.:   Great lord, unless Your Majesty tries
          to check the tumult that has arisen,
          and is spreading from one faction to another,
          dividing groups in the streets and squares,
          you will see your kingdom afloat on scarlet

nadar, entre la púrpura teñido
de su sangre, que ya con triste modo,
todo es desdichas y tragedias todo.
    Tanta es la ruina de tu imperio, tanta
la fuerza del rigor duro y sangriento,
que visto admira y escuchado espanta.
El sol se turba y se embaraza el viento;
cada piedra una pirámide levanta,
y cada flor construye un monumento,
cada edificio es un sepulcro altivo,
cada soldado un esqueleto vivo.

Sale CLOTALDO.

CLO.:   ¡Gracias a Dios que vivo a tus pies llego!
BAS.:   Clotaldo, ¿pues qué hay de Segismundo?
CLO.:   Que el vulgo, monstruo despeñado y ciego,
la torre penetró, y de lo profundo
de ella sacó su príncipe, que luego
que vio segunda vez su honor segundo,
valiente se mostró, diciendo fiero,
que ha de sacar al cielo verdadero.
BAS.:   Dadme un caballo, porque yo en persona
vencer valiente a un hijo ingrato quiero;
y en la defensa ya de mi corona,
lo que la ciencia erró, venza el acero.   (*Vase.*)
EST.:   Pues yo al lado del sol seré Belona;
poner mi nombre junto al suyo espero,
que he de volar sobre tendidas alas
a competir con la deidad de Palas. (*Vase, y tocan al arma.*)

Sale ROSAURA, *y detiene a* CLOTALDO.

ROS.:   Aunque el valor que se encierra
en tu pecho, desde allí
da voces, óyeme a mí,
que yo sé que todo es guerra.
    Ya sabes que yo llegué
pobre, humilde y desdichada
a Polonia, y amparada
de tu valor, en ti hallé

waves, dyed with the purple
of its blood, for already, in sad fashion,
all is misfortune and all is tragedy.
    So dire is the ruin of your realm, so great
the strength of severe and bloody harshness,
that it astonishes the viewer and terrifies the listener.
The sun is perturbed, and the wind is confused;
every stone erects a funerary pyramid,
and every flower builds a mausoleum,
every building is a haughty tomb,
every soldier a living skeleton.

Enter CLOTALDO.

CLO.:   Thank God that I have come to your feet alive!
BAS.:   Clotaldo, what's the news of Segismundo?
CLO.:   That the commoners, like a blind monster rushing headlong,
          have broken into the tower, and from its deeps
          have released their prince, who, the moment
          he found himself prospering a second time,
          displayed his valor, fiercely stating
          that he aims to make heaven's prediction come true.
BAS.:   Give me a horse, because I in person
          wish to overcome bravely a disloyal son;
          and, now that I am defending my crown,
          let my steel conquer where my astrology erred!   (*Exit.*)
EST.:   Then, at the side of the sun, I shall be Bellona;[31]
          I hope to set my name beside his,
          for I shall fly on outstretched wings
          to vie with the goddess Pallas!   (*Exit. An alarm sounds.*)

Enter ROSAURA, *who detains* CLOTALDO.

ROS.:   Although the valor enclosed
          in your breast cries out
          from there, listen to me,
          because I know that all is war.
              You already know that I arrived
          poor, humble, and unfortunate
          in Poland, where, protected
          by your merit, I found

---

31. Ancient Roman goddess of war.

piedad; mandásteme (¡ay cielos!)
que disfrazada viviese
en palacio, y pretendiese
(disimulando mis celos),
   guardarme de Astolfo. En fin
él me vio, y tanto atropella
mi honor, que viéndome, a Estrella
de noche habla en un jardín;
   de éste la llave he tomado,
y te podré dar lugar
de que en él puedas entrar
a dar fin a mi cuidado.
   Así, altivo, osado y fuerte
volver por mi honor podrás,
pues que ya resuelto estás
a vengarme con su muerte.

CLO.:   Verdad es que me incliné,
desde el punto que te vi,
a hacer, Rosaura, por ti
(testigo tu llanto fue)
   cuanto mi vida pudiese.
Lo primero que intenté,
quitarte aquel traje fue;
porque, si Astolfo te viese
   te viese en tu propio traje,
sin juzgar a liviandad
la loca temeridad
que hace del honor ultraje.
   En este tiempo trazaba
cómo cobrar se pudiese
tu honor perdido, aunque fuese,
tanto tu honor me arrestaba,
   dando muerte a Astolfo. ¡Mira
qué caduco desvarío!
Si bien, no siendo rey mío,
ni me asombra ni me admira.
   Darle pensé muerte, cuando
Segismundo pretendió
dármela a mí, y él llegó,

compassion in you; you ordered me (ah, heavens!)
to live under a false name
in the palace, and to try
(concealing my jealousy)
to avoid meeting Astolfo. Finally
he saw me, and he tramples my honor
to such an extent that, after seeing me, he still converses
with Estrella in a garden at night;
I have taken the key to it,
and I can give you the opportunity
to enter it
and put an end to my troubles.
In that way, proudly, boldly, and strongly,
you will be able to redress the affront to my honor,
since you are already resolved
to avenge me by his death.

CLO.:   It's true that I was inclined,
from the moment I met you,
Rosaura, to do for you
(your tears were witness to it)
all that lay in my power.
The first thing I tried
was to make you take off those men's garments;
so that, if Astolfo did see you,
he'd see you in your own clothing,
and wouldn't consider as wantonness
the mad rashness
that outrages honor.
At that time I was planning
how I could restore
your lost honor, even though it meant
(your honor was of such concern to me)
killing Astolfo. See
what a transitory folly[32] that was!
Although, since he wasn't my king,
I wasn't awe-struck or amazed.
I thought about causing his death, when
Segismundo attempted
to cause mine, and he arrived,

---

32. Or: "folly of a decrepit old man."

su peligro atropellando,
a hacer en defensa mía
muestras de su voluntad,
que fueron temeridad,
pasando de valentía.
   ¿Pues cómo yo ahora, advierte,
teniendo alma agradecida
a quien me ha dado la vida
le tengo de dar la muerte?
   Y así, entre los dos partido
el afecto y el cuidado,
viendo que a ti te la he dado,
y que de él la he recibido,
   no sé a qué parte acudir:
no sé qué parte ayudar,
si a ti me obligué con dar,
de él lo estoy con recibir;
   y así, en la acción que se ofrece,
nada a mi amor satisface,
porque soy persona que hace,
y persona que padece.

ROS.:   No tengo que prevenir
que en un varón singular,
cuanto es noble acción el dar,
es bajeza el recibir.
   Y este principio asentado,
no has de estarle agradecido,
supuesto que si él ha sido
el que la vida te ha dado,
   y tú a mí, evidente cosa
es, que él forzó tu nobleza
a que hiciese una bajeza,
y yo una acción generosa.
   Luego estás de él ofendido,
luego estás de mí obligado,
supuesto que a mí me has dado
lo que de él has recibido;
   y así debes acudir
a mi honor en riesgo tanto,
pues yo le prefiero, cuanto
va de dar a recibir.

disregarding his own peril,
   to display in my defense
his good will,
exhibiting a boldness
that went beyond mere bravery.
   So, give me heed, how can I now,
with my grateful soul,
cause the death
of the man who gave me life?
   And so, with my affection
and concern divided between the two of you,
since I have given life to you
and received it from him,
   I don't know which side to support;
I don't know which side to assist,
since I am under obligation to you for giving you life,
and to him for receiving it;
   and so, in the present emergency,
nothing can satisfy my love,
because I am both the active party
and the passive party.

Ros.:   I don't need to be the first to tell you
that, for an eminent man,
if giving is a noble action,
receiving is base to the same extent.
   And, that principle having been established,
you have no cause to be grateful to him,
because if it was he
who gave life to you,
   and you to me, it's perfectly
clear that he compelled your noble nature
to perform a base act,
whereas I led you to a magnanimous one.
   Thus, you've been offended by him;
thus, you're obliged to me,
because you gave me
what you received from him;
   and so you ought to come to the aid
of my honor in such a perilous situation,
since I excel him as much as
giving excels receiving.

CLO.:   Aunque la nobleza vive
de la parte del que da,
el agradecerla está
de parte del que recibe.
        Y pues ya dar he sabido,
ya tengo con nombre honroso
el nombre de generoso,
déjame el de agradecido,
        pues le puedo conseguir,
siendo agradecido, cuanto
liberal, pues honra tanto
el dar como el recibir.

ROS.:   De ti recibí la vida,
y tú mismo me dijiste
cuando la vida me diste,
que la que estaba ofendida
        no era vida: luego yo
nada de ti he recibido,
pues vida no vida ha sido
la que tu mano me dio.
        Y si debes ser primero
liberal que agradecido,
como de ti mismo he oído,
que me des la vida espero,
        que no me la has dado; y pues
el dar engrandece más,
sé antes liberal, serás
agradecido después.

CLO.:   Vencido de tu argumento,
antes liberal seré.
Yo, Rosaura, te daré
mi hacienda, y en un convento
        vive; que está bien pensado
el medio que solicito;
pues huyendo de un delito,
te recoges a un sagrado;
        que cuando tan dividido
el reino desdichas siente,
no he de ser quien las aumente
habiendo noble nacido.
        Con el remedio elegido

CLO.:   Even though nobility dwells
on the side of the giver,
gratitude for it belongs
on the side of the receiver.
And, since I have known how to give,
and I already possess honorably
the title of a magnanimous man,
let me retain that of a grateful man,
    since I am able to attain it,
being as grateful as I am
generous, because a man is honored by receiving
just as much as by giving.

ROS.:   I received life from you,
and you yourself told me,
when you gave me my life,
that life lived under the shadow of an affront
    wasn't really life; therefore I
received nothing from you,
since the life that your hand
gave me wasn't life.
And if you ought to be generous
sooner than grateful,
as I heard you yourself say,
I hope that you will give me life,
    for you haven't done so yet; and, since
giving is more ennobling,
be generous first, and you can be
grateful afterward.

CLO.:   Convinced by your reasoning,
I shall be generous first!
Rosaura, I shall give you
my property; take it and live
    in a convent; the plan
I have in mind is well thought out;
because you will be fleeing from a crime
and taking refuge in a sanctuary;
    for, when the kingdom,
so divided, is suffering misfortunes,
I must not be the one to increase them,
being of noble birth.
With the recourse I have chosen,

soy con el reino leal,
soy contigo liberal,
con Astolfo agradecido;
    y así escoge el que te cuadre,
quedándose entre los dos;
que no hiciera ¡vive Dios!
más, cuando fuera tu padre.

Ros.:   Cuando tú mi padre fueras,
sufriera esa injuria yo;
pero no siéndolo, no.

Clo.:   ¿Pues qué es lo que hacer esperas?

Ros.:   Matar al duque.

Clo.:   ¿Una dama,
que padres no ha conocido,
tanto valor ha tenido?

Ros.:   Sí.

Clo.:   ¿Quién te alienta?

Ros.:   Mi fama.

Clo.:   Mira que a Astolfo has de ver . . .

Ros.:   Todo mi honor lo atropella.

Clo.:   . . . tu rey, y esposo de Estrella.

Ros.:   ¡Vive Dios que no ha de ser!

Clo.:   Es locura.

Ros.:   Ya lo veo.

Clo.:   Pues véncela.

Ros.:   No podré.

Clo.:   Pues perderás . . .

Ros.:   Ya lo sé.

Clo.:   . . . vida y honor.

Ros.:   Bien lo creo.

Clo.:   ¿Qué intentas?

Ros.:   Mi muerte.

Clo.:   Mira
que eso es despecho.

Ros.:   Es honor.

Clo.:   Es desatino.

Ros.:   Es valor.

Clo.:   Es frenesí.

Ros.:   Es rabia, es ira.

I am loyal to the kingdom,
I am generous to you,
and grateful to Astolfo;
    and so, choose the plan that suits you,
which will remain a secret just between the two of us;
because, as God lives, I couldn't do
more if I were your father!

Ros.:   If you were my father,
I'd put up with this insult;
but, since you're not, I won't!

Clo.:   Then, what do you expect to do?

Ros.:   To kill the duke.

Clo.:   Is a woman
who doesn't know who her father was
so valorous?

Ros.:   Yes.

Clo.:   What spurs you on?

Ros.:   My reputation.

Clo.:   Remember that you will see Astolfo . . .

Ros.:   He tramples on all my honor.

Clo.:   . . . as your king, and husband of Estrella.

Ros.:   As God lives, it will never happen!

Clo.:   This is madness.

Ros.:   I can see that.

Clo.:   Then, overcome it.

Ros.:   I can't!

Clo.:   Then you'll lose . . .

Ros.:   I know.

Clo.:   . . . both life and honor.

Ros.:   I believe so.

Clo.:   What are you aiming at?

Ros.:   My death.

Clo.:   Observe
that this is spitefulness.[33]

Ros.:   It's a sense of honor.

Clo.:   It's folly.

Ros.:   It's a sense of worth.

Clo.:   It's frenzy.

Ros.:   It's rage, it's anger.

---

33. Or: "desperation."

CLO.:   En fin, ¿que no se da medio
               a tu ciega pasión?
ROS.:   No.
CLO.:   ¿Quién ha de ayudarte?
ROS.:   Yo.
CLO.:   ¿No hay remedio?
ROS.:   No hay remedio.
CLO.:   Piensa bien si hay otros modos . . .
ROS.:   Perderme de otra manera.
CLO.:   Pues si has de perderte, espera,
               hija, y perdámonos todos.   (*Vase.*)

               Tocan y salen marchando SOLDADOS,
               CLARÍN *y* SEGISMUNDO *vestido de pieles.*

SEG.:   Si este día me viera
               Roma en los triunfos de su edad primera,
                  ¡oh, cuánto se alegrara
               viendo lograr una ocasión tan rara
                  de tener una fiera
               que sus grandes ejércitos rigiera;
                  a cuyo altivo aliento
               fuera poca conquista el firmamento!
               Pero el vuelo abatamos,
               espíritu, no así desvanezcamos
                  aqueste aplauso incierto,
               si ha de pesarme, cuando esté despierto,
                  de haberlo conseguido
               para haberlo perdido;
                  pues mientras menos fuere,
               menos se sentirá si se perdiere.

               Dentro un clarín.

CLA.:   En un veloz caballo
               (perdóname, que fuerza es el pintallo
                  en viniéndome a cuento),
               en quien un mapa se dibuja atento,
                  pues el cuerpo es la tierra,
               el fuego el alma que en el pecho encierra,
                  la espuma el mar, el aire su suspiro,
               en cuya confusión un caos admiro;
                  pues en el alma, espuma, cuerpo, aliento,

CLO.:   So finally, there's no refraining
          your blind emotion?
ROS.:   No!
CLO.:   Who can help you?
ROS.:   Myself.
CLO.:   Is there no recourse?
ROS.:   There is no recourse.
CLO.:   Think hard and see if there are other ways . . .
ROS.:   To ruin myself in another fashion!
CLO.:   Well, if you must ruin yourself, wait,
          my girl, and let's all ruin ourselves.   (*They exit.*)

Trumpets blow, and SOLDIERS *march in with* CLARÍN
and with SEGISMUNDO, *who is dressed in animal skins.*

SEG.:   If Rome in the triumphs
          of its golden age could see me today,
              oh, how happy it would be
          to gain such a rare opportunity:
              to have a wild animal
          leading its mighty armies;
              for whose proud zeal
          the firmament would be a petty conquest!
              But let us fly at a lower height,
          my spirit, lest we thus dispel
              this dubious acclamation,
          in case I am to be grieved, once I'm awake,
              at having attained it
          only to lose it again;
              since, the slighter it is,
          the less I'll regret it if I lose it.

A clarion sounds within.

CLA.:   On a swift steed
          (forgive me, because I must depict it
              when I find it opportune),
          on which a careful map is drawn—
              because its body is the earth,
          the soul contained in its breast is fire,
              its froth is the sea, its breath is air,
          in the mingling of all of which I marvel at seeing a chaos;
              since in its soul, foam, body, and breath,

monstruo es de fuego, tierra, mar y viento,
de color remendado,
rucio, y a su propósito rodado
del que bate la espuela,
y en vez de correr vuela;
a tu presencia llega
airosa una mujer.

SEG.:   Su luz me ciega.

CLA.:   ¡Vive Dios, que es Rosaura!   (*Vase.*)

SEG.:   El cielo a mi presencia la restaura.

Sale ROSAURA *con baquero, espada y daga.*

ROS.:   Generoso Segismundo,
cuya majestad heroica
sale al día de sus hechos
de la noche de sus sombras;
y como el mayor planeta,
que en los brazos de la aurora
se restituye luciente
a las flores y a las rosas,
y sobre mares y montes
cuando coronado asoma,
luz esparce, rayos brilla,
cumbres baña, espumas borda;
así amanezcas al mundo,
luciente sol de Polonia,
que a una mujer infelice,
que hoy a tus plantas se arroja,
ampares por ser mujer
y desdichada: dos cosas,
que para obligar a un hombre
que de valiente blasona,
cualquiera de las dos basta,
de las dos cualquiera sobra.
Tres veces son las que ya
me admiras, tres las que ignoras
quién soy, pues las tres me has visto
en diverso traje y forma.

it is a hybrid of fire, earth, sea, and wind—
    a horse of patchy color,
gray, and broken in[34] to suit the purposes
    of the one who spurs it on,
so that it flies rather than runs:
    there arrives in your presence
an elegant woman.

SEG.:   Her light blinds me.
CLA.:   As God lives, it's Rosaura!   (*Exit.*)
SEG.:   Heaven brings her back into my presence!

ROSAURA *enters, in a long, loose tunic, with sword and dagger.*

ROS.:   Noble Segismundo,
    whose heroic majesty
emerges into the day of his deeds
    out of the night of his darkness;
and, like the chief planet,
    which, in the arms of dawn,
restores itself gleamingly
    to the flowers and roses,
and, when it appears with its crown
    above seas and mountains,
sheds light, darts beams,
    bathes peaks, embroiders foaming waves:
so may you dawn upon the world,
    gleaming sun of Poland,
and may you protect an unhappy woman,
    who throws herself at your feet today,
because she is a woman
    and unfortunate; two things,
either of which is sufficient,
    either of which is more than sufficient,
to place under an obligation a man
    who boasts of being brave.
Three times now
    you have gazed on me with wonder, each time not knowing
who I am, since, each of the three times, you saw me
    in different attire and guise.

---

34. Or: "dappled." (The dappling would suit its rider by showing where to apply the spurs.)

La primera me creíste
varón en la rigurosa
prisión, donde fue tu vida
de mis desdichas lisonja.
La segunda me admiraste
mujer, cuando fue la pompa
de tu majestad un sueño,
una fantasma, una sombra.
La tercera es hoy, que siendo
monstruo de una especie y otra,
entre galas de mujer
armas de varón me adornan.
Y porque compadecido
mejor mi amparo dispongas,
es bien que de mis sucesos
trágicas fortunas oigas.
De noble madre nací
en la corte de Moscovia,
que, según fue desdichada,
debió de ser muy hermosa.
En ésta puso los ojos
un traidor, que no le nombra
mi voz por no conocerle,
de cuyo valor me informa
el mío; pues siendo objeto
de su idea, siento ahora
no haber nacido gentil,
para persuadirme loca
a que fue algún dios de aquellos
que en metamorfosis lloran
lluvia de oro, cisne y toro
Dánae, Leda y Europa.
Cuando pensé que alargaba,
citando aleves historias,
el discurso, hallo que en él
te he dicho en razones pocas
que mi madre, persuadida

The first time, you thought I
was a man, in your harsh
prison, where your mode of life
was a solace to my own misfortunes.
The second time, you beheld me
as a woman, when the pomp
of your majesty was a dream,
a ghost, a shade.
Now is the third time, when I am
a hybrid of the two sexes,
since alongside women's finery
masculine weapons adorn me.
And so that, moved to pity,
you may better prepare to protect me,
it is fitting for you to hear
the tragic fortune of my history.
I was born of a noble mother
at the court of Muscovy,
who, to correspond to her misfortune,
must have been very beautiful.
On her a deceiver
set eyes; my voice
doesn't name him because I don't know who it was,
but I am assured of his merit
by my own; because, being the result
of which he was the active cause,[35] I now regret
that I wasn't born a pagan,
so that I could persuade myself foolishly
that my father was one of those gods
who, transformed into other shapes, are bewailed,
as a rain of gold, a swan, or a bull,
by Danae, Leda, and Europa.[36]
When I thought I was protracting
my speech by mentioning
stories of treachery, I find that in it
I have informed you in very few words
that my mother, seduced

---

35. Her father was like a heavenly Platonic idea, and she is like a corresponding earthly specimen of it.   36. Zeus (Jupiter) seduced those three women in the corresponding guises mentioned in the preceding line. Some editions read *Cilene* for *Leda*, but no ancient Greek Cyllene or Selene suits the context.

a finezas amorosas,
fue, como ninguna, bella,
y fue infeliz como todas.
Aquella necia disculpa
de fe y palabra de esposa
la alcanzó tanto, que aún hoy
el pensamiento la cobra,
habiendo sido un tirano
tan Eneas de su Troya,
que la dejó hasta la espada.
Enváinese aquí su hoja,
que yo la desnudaré
antes que acabe la historia.
De este, pues, mal dado nudo
que ni ata ni aprisiona,
o matrimonio o delito
si bien todo es una cosa,
nací yo tan parecida,
que fui un retrato, una copia
ya que en la hermosura no,
en la dicha y en las obras;
y así, no habré menester
decir que poco dichosa
heredera de fortunas,
corrí con ella una propia.
Lo más que podré decirte
de mí, es el dueño que roba
los trofeos de mi honor,
los despojos de mi honra.
Astolfo . . . ¡Ay de mí! al nombrarle
se encoleriza y se enoja
el corazón, propio efeto
de que enemigo se nombra.—
Astolfo due el dueño ingrato
que olvidado de las glorias
(porque en un pasado amor
se olvida hasta la memoria),

by amorous compliments,
was beautiful like no other woman
and as unhappy as all women.
That foolish pretext—
giving his promise and word to marry her—
won her over so completely that even today
she considers herself properly wed,[37]
though he was a tyrant
so much like Trojan Aeneas[38]
that he even left her his sword.
Let its blade be sheathed here,
for I shall bare it
before my story is finished.
Well, then, from that poorly tied knot
which neither binds nor imprisons,
a marriage or a crime
(it's all the same thing),
I was born, so resembling her
that I was a portrait, a copy of her,
not in beauty
but in luck and deeds;
and so, I won't need
to say that, an unfortunate
heiress to her lot,
I had the same as hers.
The most I can tell you
about myself is about the lord and master who has stolen
the trophies of my honor,
the remains of my good name.
Astolfo . . . Woe is me! When I name him,
my heart grows angry
and irritated, the characteristic result
of naming one's enemy.—
Astolfo was that faithless master
who, forgetting our glories
(for, when a love affair is over,
even the memory of it is lost),

---

37. Or: "she regrets it." Some editions read *el pensamiento la llora* ("her mind be-
moans it [the pretext]"). 38. Who abandoned Dido of Carthage, leaving her his
sword; the Spanish partially suggests that Aeneas left behind his sword when fleeing
from the destruction of Troy, but that would be an error.

vino a Polonia, llamado
de su conquista famosa,
a casarse con Estrella,
que fue de mi ocaso antorcha.
¿Quién creerá, que habiendo sido
una estrella quien conforma
dos amantes, sea una Estrella
la que los divida ahora?
Yo ofendida, yo burlada,
quedé triste, quedé loca,
quedé muerta, quedé yo,
que es decir que quedó toda
la confusión del infierno
cifrada en mi Babilonia;
y declarándome muda
(porque hay penas y congojas
que las dicen los afectos
mucho mejor que la boca),
dije mis penas callando,
hasta que una vez a solas,
Violante mi madre (¡ay, cielos!)
rompió la prisión, y en tropa
del pecho salieron juntas,
tropezando unas con otras.
No me embaracé en decirlas;
que en sabiendo una persona
que, a quien sus flaquezas cuenta,
ha sido cómplice en otras,
parece que ya le hace
la salva y le desahoga;
que a veces el mal ejemplo
sirve de algo. En fin, piadosa
oyó mis quejas, y quiso
consolarme con las propias:
juez que ha sido delincuente,
¡qué fácilmente perdona!
Y escarmentando en sí misma,
y por negar a la ociosa

came to Poland, summoned
by a notable conquest,
to marry Estrella,
who was his guiding light while my sun was setting.
Who could believe that, after
a star brought us two lovers
together, it would be the star Estrella
who now separates them?
I, offended and scorned,
became sad, became crazed,
became a dead woman, became what I am:
that is, all the confusion
of hell became
summed up in my own Babel;
and, declaring myself wordlessly
(because there are distresses and sorrows
much better expressed
by the feelings than by the lips),
I told of my distresses in silence,
until, one time when we were alone,
my mother Violante (ah, heavens!)
broke through my prison wall, and in a throng
they all emerged from my bosom together,
one stumbling over the other.
I wasn't embarrassed to recount them,
because, when a person knows
that the one to whom he is confessing his weaknesses
has been involved in similar ones himself,
it seems as if that encourages him
to speak,[39] and relieves him;
because at times a bad example
is good for something. In short, she compassionately
heard my laments, and tried
to console me with her own:
how readily a judge pardons
when he himself has been a criminal!
And, taking a lesson from her own experience,
and unsatisfied with having left it to idle

---

39. Or: "as if that acts like an official taster" (someone who tastes the king's food to make sure it isn't poisoned).

libertad, al tiempo fácil,
el remedio de su honra,
no le tuvo en mis desdichas;
por mejor consejo toma
que le siga, y que le obligue,
con finezas prodigiosas,
a la deuda de mi honor;
y para que a menos costa
fuese, quiso mi fortuna
que en traje de hombre me ponga.
Descolgó una antigua espada
que es ésta que ciño; ahora
es tiempo que se desnude,
como prometí, la hoja.
Pues confiada en sus señas,
me dijo: "Parte a Polonia,
y procura que te vean
ese acero que te adorna,
los más nobles; que en alguno
podrá ser que hallen piadosa
acogida tus fortunas,
y consuelo tus congojas."
Llegué a Polonia, en efeto:
pasemos, pues que no importa
el decirlo, y ya se sabe,
que un bruto que se desboca
me llevó a tu cueva, adonde
tú de mirarme te asombras.
Pasemos que allí Clotaldo
de mi parte se apasiona,
que pide mi vida al rey,
que el rey mi vida le otorga;
que informado de quién soy,
me persuade a que me ponga
mi propio traje, y que sirva
a Estrella, donde ingeniosa
estorbé el amor de Astolfo
y el ser Estrella su esposa.

freedom[40] and easy-going time
to bring redress to her loss of good name,
she wanted me to act differently in my misfortunes;
she thought it was a better idea
for me to follow him, and make him acknowledge
his debt to my honor,
with miraculous displays of affection;
and, so that it might be
less difficult, my fortune decreed
that I should dress in men's clothing.
She took from the wall an old sword,
the one I'm now wearing; this
is the time for me to unsheathe
its blade, as I promised.
Because, confident it would be recognized,
she said to me: "Leave for Poland,
and try to have the greatest noblemen
catch sight of the steel
that adorns you; because, perhaps,
in one of them your fortunes
may find a compassionate welcome,
and your sorrows consolation."
I did indeed arrive in Poland:
let us omit the fact, since it's not important
to relate it, and it's already known,
that the bolting of my horse
brought me to your cave, where
you were amazed to see me.
Let us omit the fact that there Clotaldo
took my part warmly,
that he asked the king to spare my life,
that the king granted him my life;
that, when Clotaldo learned who I was,
he persuaded me to put on
my own normal clothing and to become a servant
to Estrella; doing so, I cleverly
broke up Astolfo's romance
and his marriage to Estrella.

---

40. The carefree ways of the seducer, or idleness on the part of the seduced? The whole passage, from *Y escarmentando* to *mis desdichas*, is problematic and has been interpreted in various ways.

Pasemos que aquí me viste
otra vez confuso, y otra
con el traje de mujer
confundiste entrambas formas,
y vamos a que Clotaldo,
persuadido a que le importa
que se casen y que reinen
Astolfo y Estrella hermosa,
contra mi honor me aconseja
que la pretensión deponga.
Yo, viendo que tú ¡oh, valiente
Segismundo! a quien hoy toca
la venganza, pues el cielo
quiere que la cárcel rompas
de esa rústica prisión,
donde ha sido tu persona
al sentimiento una fiera,
al sufrimiento una roca,
las armas contra tu patria
y contra tu padre tomas,
vengo a ayudarte, mezclando
entre las galas costosas
de Diana, los arneses
de Palas, vistiendo ahora
ya la tela y ya el acero,
que entrambos juntos me adornan.
Ea, pues, fuerte caudillo,
a los dos juntos importa
impedir y deshacer
estas concertadas bodas:
a mí, porque no se case
el que mi esposo se nombra,
y a ti, porque, estando juntos
sus dos estados, no pongan
con más poder y más fuerza
en duda nuestra victoria.
Mujer vengo a persuadirte
al remedio de mi honra,
y varón vengo a alentarte

Let us omit the fact that here you saw me
once again in your confusion, and that, that time,
when I was wearing women's clothes,
you mixed up my two appearances in your mind;
and let us proceed to the moment when Clotaldo,
convinced that it was essential to him
for Astolfo and beautiful Estrella
to wed and reign,
advised me, to the detriment of my honor,
to relinquish my claim.
When I saw that you, brave
Segismundo, whose turn it is
for revenge today—since heaven
wishes you to break out of the confinement
of this mean prison,
where you have been
a wild animal to your feelings,
and a rock to your suffering—
were taking arms against
your country and your father,
I came to aid you, adding
to the expensive finery
of Diana[41] the armor
of Pallas, and now wearing
both fine fabrics and steel,
which adorn me together.
Onward, then, brave chieftain,
it behooves the two of us together
to prevent and dissolve
this wedding that has been planned:
it behooves me, so that the man I call
my husband doesn't wed,
and you, so that, when their two dominions
are joined, they will not make
our victory doubtful
with their greater power and strength.
As a woman, I have come to urge you
to restore my good name;
as a man, I have come to spur you on

---

41. The chaste goddess of the hunt.

a que cobres tu corona.
Mujer vengo a enternecerte
cuando a tus plantas me ponga
y varón vengo a servirte
cuando a tus gentes socorra.
Mujer vengo a que me valgas
en mi agravio y mi congoja,
y varón vengo a valerte
con mi acero y mi persona.
Y así piensa, que si hoy
como a mujer me enamoras
como varón te daré
la muerte en defensa honrosa
de mi honor, porque he de ser
en su conquista amorosa,
mujer para darte quejas,
varón para ganar honras.

SEG.:   Cielos, si es verdad que sueño,
suspendedme la memoria,
que no es posible que quepan
en un sueño tantas cosas.
¡Válgame Dios, quién supiera,
o saber salir de todas,
o no pensar en ninguna!
¿Quién vio penas tan dudosas?
Si soñé aquella grandeza
en que me vi, ¿cómo ahora
esta mujer me refiere
unas señas tan notorias?
Luego fue verdad, no sueño;
y si fue verdad, que es otra
confusión y no menor,
¿cómo mi vida le nombra
sueño? ¿Pues tan parecidas
a los sueños son las glorias,
que las verdaderas son
tenidas por mentirosas,
y las fingidas por ciertas?
¿Tan poco hay de unas a otras,
que hay cuestión sobre saber
si lo que se ve y se goza,

to recover your crown.
As a woman, I have come to soften your heart
by throwing myself at your feet;
as a man, I have come to serve you
by aiding your army.
As a woman, I have come for you to help me
in my affront and sorrow;
as a man, I have come to stand by you
with my steel and my body.
And so, believe me: if today
you make love to me as to a woman,
as a man I shall
kill you in dignified defense
of my honor, because in this
love-war I shall be
a woman to lament to you,
and a man to win a reputation.

SEG.: Heavens, if I'm really dreaming,
let my mind cease working now,
because it's impossible for so many things
to be contained in one dream!
God help me, if I could only
escape them all
or not think of any of them!
Who ever beheld such painful uncertainty?
If I only dreamed that grandeur
in which I found myself, how then now
can this woman mention
such accurate details?
Then, it was reality, not a dream;
and, if it was reality—which only adds
to the confusion, and doesn't lessen it—
how can I call it
a dream? Are glories, then,
so similar to dreams
that real ones
are considered fictitious
and feigned ones true?
Is there so little difference between them
that it's questionable knowledge
whether what one sees and enjoys

es mentira o es verdad?
¿Tan semejante es la copia
al original, que hay duda
en saber si es ella propia?
Pues si es así, y ha de verse
desvanecida entre sombras
la grandeza y el poder,
la majestad y la pompa,
sepamos aprovechar
este rato que nos toca,
pues sólo se goza en ella
lo que entre sueños se goza.
Rosaura está en mi poder,
su hermosura el alma adora,
gocemos, pues, la ocasión,
el amor las leyes rompa
del valor y confianza
con que a mis plantas se postra.
Esto es sueño, y pues lo es
soñemos dichas ahora
que después serán pesares.
Mas ¡con mis razones propias
vuelvo a convencerme a mí!
Si es sueño, si es vanagloria,
¿quién, por vanagloria humana,
pierde una divina gloria?
¿Qué pasado bien no es sueño?
¿Quién tuvo dichas heroicas
que entre sí no diga, cuando
las revuelve en su memoria:
sin duda que fue soñado
cuanto vi? Pues si esto toca
mi desengaño, si sé
que es el gusto llama hermosa,
que la convierte en cenizas
cualquiera viento que sopla,
acudamos a lo eterno,
que es la fama vividora
donde ni duermen las dichas,
ni las grandezas reposan.
Rosaura está sin honor;

is a lie or the truth?
Is the copy so similar
to the original that doubt arises
as to which is which?
Then, if that's the case, and we are fated to see
grandeur and power,
majesty and pomp,
dispersed in the darkness,
let us learn how to make good use
of this brief time allotted to us,
because all we enjoy in real life
is what we enjoy in dreams!
Rosaura is in my power,
my soul worships her beauty;
so let us enjoy the opportunity;
let love violate the laws
of that merit and trust
which cause her to prostrate herself at my feet!
This is a dream, and, since it is,
let us now dream of happiness
that will be sorrow later on!
But, I convince myself of the opposite
with my own reasoning!
If it's a dream, if it's vainglory,
who, in exchange for human vainglory,
would lose a divine glory?
What bygone happiness isn't a dream?
Who that has ever had heroic good fortune
hasn't said to himself, when
his memory reverted to it:
"Without a doubt, everything I saw
was a dream"? Well, if this is a cause for
my becoming disillusioned, if I know
that pleasure is a lovely flame
that is turned to ashes
by any wind that blows,
let us look to eternity,
which is everlasting fame
where good fortune does not sleep
and grandeur does not take repose!
Rosaura has lost her honor;

más a un príncipe le toca
el dar honor, que quitarle.
¡Vive Dios! que de su honra
he de ser conquistador,
antes que de mi corona.
Huyamos de la ocasión,
que es muy fuerte.—Al arma toca,
que hoy he de dar la batalla,
antes que las negras sombras
sepulten los rayos de oro
entre verdinegras ondas.

ROS.:   ¡Señor! ¿pues así te ausentas?
¿Pues ni una palabra sola
no te debe mi cuidado,
no merece mi congoja?
¿Cómo es posible, señor,
que ni me mires ni oigas?
¿Aún no me vuelves el rostro?

SEG.:   Rosaura, al honor le importa,
por ser piadoso contigo,
ser cruel contigo ahora.
No te responde mi voz,
porque mi honor te responda;
no te hablo, porque quiero
que te hablen por mí mis obras,
ni te miro, porque es fuerza,
en pena tan rigurosa,
que no mire tu hermosura
quien ha de mirar tu honra.   (Vanse.)

ROS.:   ¿Qué enigmas, cielos, son éstas?
Después de tanto pesar,
¡aún me queda que dudar
con equívocas respuestas!

Sale CLARÍN.

CLA.:   ¿Señora, es hora de verte?
ROS.:   ¡Ay, Clarín! ¿dónde has estado?
CLA.:   En una torre encerrado
brujuleando mi muerte,
     si me da, o . . . no me da;
y a figura que me diera,

it is more befitting a prince
to give honor than to take it away.
As God lives, I shall be
the restorer of her good name
before I recover my own crown!
Let us flee this opportunity,
which is so tempting.—Sound the alarm,
for I mean to give battle today
before the black shadows
bury the sun's golden beams
in the dark-green waters!

Ros.: Sire! Don't tell me you're going away like this!
Doesn't my anguish require,
doesn't my sorrow deserve,
at least one word from you?
How is it possible, Sire,
that you neither look at me nor listen to me?
You still won't turn your face to me?

SEG.: Rosaura, it is essential to honor,
if I am to compassionate with you,
to be cruel to you now.
My voice doesn't answer you,
so that my honor *can;*
I don't speak to you, because I want
my actions to speak to you for me;
I don't look at you because, of necessity,
in such severe distress,
the man who must look to your honor
mustn't look at your beauty.   (*Exit, with* SOLDIERS.)

Ros.: Heaven, what is this riddle?
After so much suffering,
I'm still left in doubt
by ambiguous replies!

Enter CLARÍN.

CLA.: My lady, is this a good time to talk to you?
Ros.: Alas, Clarín, where have you been?
CLA.: Locked in a tower,
examining my hand at cards to see
whether or not they spelt death;
and, if I were dealt a court card,

	pasante quínola fuera	
	mi vida: que estuve ya	
	para dar un estallido.	

Ros.:   ¿Por qué?

Cla.:   Porque sé el secreto
            de quién eres, y en efeto
            Clotaldo . . . ¿Pero qué ruido   (*Dentro cajas*)
            es éste?

Ros.:   ¿Qué puede ser?

Cla.:   Que del palacio sitiado
            sale un escuadrón armado
            a resistir y vencer
                el del fiero Segismundo.

Ros.:   ¿Pues cómo cobarde estoy,
            y ya a su lado no soy
            un escándalo del mundo,
                cuando ya tanta crueldad
            cierra sin orden ni ley?   (*Vase.*)

Unos: ¡Viva nuestro invicto rey!   (*Dentro.*)

Otros: ¡Viva nuestra libertad!   (*Dentro.*)

Cla.:   ¡La libertad y el rey vivan!
            Vivan muy enhorabuena,
            que a mí nada me da pena
            como en cuenta me reciban;
                que yo, apartado este día
            en tan grande confusión,
            haga el papel de Nerón,
            que de nada se dolía.
                Si bien me quiero doler
            de algo, y ha de ser de mí:
            escondido, desde aquí
            toda la fiesta he de ver.
                El sitio es oculto y fuerte,
            entre estas peñas; pues ya
            la muerte no me hallará,
            dos higas para la muerte.   (*Escóndese.*)

a perfect flush[42] would have
saved my life; and I was all ready
to explode.

ROS.:   Why?

CLA.:   Because I know the truth
about you, and in fact
Clotaldo . . . [*Drums within.*] But what
is that sound?

ROS.:   What can it be?

CLA.:   It means that from the besieged palace
an armed squadron is making a sortie
to resist and overcome
fierce Segismundo's squadron.

ROS.:   Then why am I standing here like a coward,
and not at his side,
like a shock to the world,
now that so much cruelty
is closing in without order or system?   (*Exit.*)

VOICES (*within*):   Long live our unconquered king!

OTHERS (*within*):   Long live our liberty!

CLA.:   Long live liberty *and* the king!
May they live very happily,
because I don't care at all
as long as I'm taken good care of;
for I shall step off to the side on this day
of such great confusion,
to play the role of Nero,
who wasn't concerned about anything.[43]
If there's one thing I want to be
concerned about, it's myself:
in hiding, from this vantage point
I'll be able to see the whole show.
The spot is concealed and protected,
between these rocks; and, since now
death won't find me,
two figs for death!   (*He hides.*)

---

42. No doubt, the Spanish original contains puns relative to terminology in the card game *quínola*, in which four-of-a-kind was a winning hand. 43. He "fiddled while Rome burned."

Suena ruido de armas. Salen el REY [BASILIO],
CLOTALDO *y* ASTOLFO, *huyendo.*

BAS.:   ¿Hay más infelice rey?
        ¿Hay padre más perseguido?
CLO.:   Ya tu ejército vencido
        baja sin tino ni ley.
AST.:   Los traidores vencedores
        quedan.
BAS.:   En batallas tales
        los que vencen son leales,
        los vencidos los traidores.
        Huyamos, Clotaldo, pues,
        del cruel, del inhumano
        rigor de un hijo tirano.

            Disparan dentro y cae CLARÍN, *herido,*
                    de donde está.

BAS.:   ¡Válgame el cielo!
AST.:   ¿Quién es
        este infelice soldado,
        que a nuestros pies ha caído
        en sangre todo teñido?
CLA.:   Soy un hombre desdichado,
            que por quererme guardar
        de la muerte, la busqué.
        Huyendo de ella, topé
        con ella, pues no hay lugar,
            para la muerte secreto;
        de donde claro se arguye
        que quien más su efeto huye,
        es quien se llega a su efeto.
            Por eso, tornad, tornad
        a la lid sangrienta luego,
        que entre las armas y el fuego
        hay mayor seguridad
            que en el monte más guardado,
        pues no hay seguro camino
        a la fuerza del destino
        y a la inclemencia del hado;
            y así, aunque a libraros vais

The sound of weapons. Enter King BASILIO, CLOTALDO,
and ASTOLFO, *in retreat.*

BAS.: Is there an unluckier king?
Is there a more persecuted father?

CLO.: Your beaten army is now
descending without order or common sense.

AST.: The traitors remain
the victors.

BAS.: In such battles
the winners are the loyal ones,
the losers are the traitors.
So let us flee, Clotaldo,
from the cruel, inhuman
harshness of a tyrannical son!

Shots are fired within and CLARÍN, *wounded,*
falls out of his hiding place.

BAS.: Heaven help me!

AST.: Who is
this unlucky soldier
who has fallen at our feet
all dyed in blood?

CLA.: I'm an unfortunate man,
who, in trying to guard myself
from death, sought it out.
Fleeing from it, I ran
into it, because there is no place
where you can hide from death;
the obvious conclusion from this
is that the man who tries hardest to escape its workings
is the one who makes them come about.
Therefore, go back, go back
at once to the bloody conflict,
because amid the weapons and fire
there is greater safety
than on the most protected mountain,
since there's no path safe against
the force of destiny
and the inclemency of fate;
and so, even if you try to escape

      de la muerte con huir,
      mirad que vais a morir
      si está de Dios que muráis.   (*Cae dentro.*)
BAS.:   ¡Mirad que vais a morir
      si está de Dios que muráis!
      ¡Qué bien (¡ay cielos!) persuade
      nuestro error, nuestra ignorancia,
      a mayor conocimiento
      este cadáver que habla
      por la boca de una herida
      siendo el humor que desata
      sangrienta lengua que enseña
      que son diligencias vanas
      del hombre, cuantas dispone
      contra mayor fuerza y causa!
      Pues yo, por librar de muertes
      y sediciones mi patria,
      vine a entregarla a los mismos
      de quien pretendí librarla.
CLO.:   Aunque el hado, señor, sabe
      todos los caminos, y halla
      a quien busca entre lo espeso
      de las peñas, no es cristiana
      determinación decir
      que no hay reparo a su saña.
      Sí hay, que el prudente varón
      vitoria del hado alcanza;
      y si no estás reservado
      de la pena y la desgracia,
      haz por donde te reserves.
AST.:   Clotaldo, señor, te habla
      como prudente varón
      que madura edad alcanza;
      yo como joven valiente:
      entre las espesas ramas
      de ese monte está un caballo,
      veloz aborto del aura;
      huye en él, que yo, entretanto,
      te guardaré las espaldas.
BAS.:   Si está de Dios que yo muera,
      o si la muerte me aguarda

death by running away,
you can be sure that you will die
if it's God's will that you die.   (*He falls offstage and dies*).

BAS.:   "You can be sure that you will die
if it's God's will that you die!"
Ah, heavens! How eloquently our folly,
our ignorance, are taught
surer knowledge
by this corpse that speaks
through the lips of a wound,
the fluid that he emits being
a tongue of blood to teach us
that every effort man makes
against a greater force and cause
is in vain!
For I, to free my country
from murders and uprisings,
have finally handed it over to the very things
from which I tried to free it.

CLO.:   Sire, even though fate knows
every pathway and finds
the man it seeks amid the thickness
of rocks, it isn't a Christian
belief to say
that there's no protection against its fury.
There is, for the man with foresight
can gain victory over fate;
and, if you are not yet secure
against distress and misfortune,
create that security for yourself.

AST.:   Sire, Clotaldo speaks to you
like a wise man
who has reached maturity;
I, like a brave youngster:
amid the dense branches
of this mountain there is a horse,
a swift hybrid offspring of the wind;
escape on it, while in the meantime
I guard your rear.

BAS.:   If it's God's will that I die,
or if death lurks for me

aquí, hoy la quiero buscar,
esperando cara a cara.

Tocan al arma y sale SEGISMUNDO
y toda la compañía.

SOLDADO: En lo intrincado del monte,
entre sus espesas ramas,
el rey se esconde.
SEG.:   ¡Seguilde!
No quede en sus cumbres planta
que no examine el cuidado,
tronco a tronco, y rama a rama.
CLO.:   ¡Huye, señor!
BAS.:   ¿Para qué?
AST.:   ¿Qué intentas?
BAS.:   Astolfo, aparta.
CLO.:   ¿Qué quieres?
BAS.:   Hacer, Clotaldo
un remedio que me falta.—
Si a mí buscándome vas
ya estoy, príncipe, a tus plantas;
sea de ellas blanca alfombra
esta nieve de mis canas.
Pisa mi cerviz, y huella
mi corona; postra, arrastra
mi decoro y mi respeto,
toma de mi honor venganza,
sírvete de mí cautivo
y tras prevenciones tantas,
cumpla el hado su homenaje,
cumpla el cielo su palabra.
SEG.:   Corte ilustre de Polonia,
que de admiraciones tantas
sois testigos, atended
que vuestro príncipe os habla.
Lo que está determinado
del cielo, y en azul tabla
Dios con el dedo escribió
de quien son cifras y estampas
tantos papeles azules
que adornan letras doradas,

here, I wish to seek it today,
awaiting it face to face.

An alarm sounds and SEGISMUNDO *enters*
with all the other characters [who are still alive].

SOLDIER: In the tangle of the mountain,
amid its dense branches,
the king is hiding.
SEG.:   Follow him!
Let no tree remain on its heights
that is not carefully searched,
trunk by trunk, bough by bough.
CLO.:   Flee, Sire!
BAS.:   To what end?
AST.:   What do you have in mind?
BAS.:   Astolfo, step aside.
CLO.:   What do you want to do?
BAS.:   Clotaldo, to try
a recourse that I haven't attempted yet.—
If you're looking for me,
Prince, I am now at your feet;
let this snow of my hair
be a white carpet for them.
Tread on my neck, and step on
my crown; topple and drag
my dignity and the respect due me,
take revenge on my honor,
treat me as your captive,
and, after all those preventive measures,
let fate receive its homage,
let heaven keep its word!
SEG.:   Illustrious court of Poland,
you who are witness to such great
marvels, be attentive,
for it's your prince addressing you.
That which is decided on
in heaven, and which on its blue chart
God has written with His finger
(of which all those blue sheets
adorned with gold letters
are the emblems and signs),

nunca engañan, nunca mienten;
porque quien miente y engaña
es quien, para usar mal de ellas,
las penetra y las alcanza.
Mi padre, que está presente
por excusarse a la saña
de mi condición, me hizo
un bruto, una fiera humana;
de suerte, que cuando yo
por mi nobleza gallarda,
por mi sangre generosa,
por mi condición bizarra
hubiera nacido dócil
y humilde, sólo bastara
tal género de vivir,
tal linaje de crianza,
a hacer fieras mis costumbres:
¡qué buen modo de estorbarlas!
Si a cualquier hombre dijesen:
"Alguna fiera inhumana
te dará muerte" ¿escogiera
buen remedio en despertallas
cuando estuviesen durmiendo?
Si dijeran: "Esta espada
que traes ceñida ha de ser
quien te dé la muerte"; vana
diligencia de evitarlo
fuera entonces desnudarla
y ponérsela a los pechos.
Si dijesen: "Golfos de agua
han de ser tu sepultura
en monumentos de plata";
mal hiciera en darse al mar,
cuando soberbio levanta
rizados montes de nieve,
de cristal crespas montañas.
Lo mismo le ha sucedido
que a quien, porque le amenaza
una fiera, la despierta;
que a quien, temiendo una espada,
la desnuda; y que a quien mueve

never deceives, never lies;
because the one who lies and deceives
is the man who understands
and interprets them to make bad use of them.
My father, here present,
to exempt himself from the rabid fury
of my nature, made me
an animal, a human beast;
so that, whereas,
through my gallant nobility of birth,
through my highminded heredity,
through my generous nature,
I might have been born tractable
and humble, all that was needed
was that way of life,
that sort of upbringing,
to make my manners fierce:
what a fine way to counteract them!
If any man were told:
"Some inhuman beast
will kill you," would he be choosing
the proper protection by awakening them
when they were sleeping?
If he were told: "That sword
you're wearing will be
the one that kills you," it would then be
an incorrect countermeasure
to unsheathe it
and point it at his breast.
If he were told: "Gulfs of water
will be your grave
with the waves as silver-tinted gravestones,"
he would do wrong to set out to sea
when it haughtily raises
curling mountains of snowy foam,
rippling hills of crystal.
The same thing has happened to him
as to the man who awakened
a wild animal because it threatened him;
the man, who, fearing a sword,
unsheathed it; and the man who stirred up

las ondas de una borrasca;
y cuando fuera (escuchadme)
dormida fiera mi saña,
templada espada mi furia,
mi rigor, quieta bonanza,
la fortuna no se vence
con injusticia y venganza,
porque antes se incita más;
y así, quien vencer aguarda
a su fortuna, ha de ser
con prudencia y con templanza.
No antes de venir el daño
se reserva ni se guarda
quien le previene; que aunque
puede humilde (cosa es clara)
reservarse de él, no es
sino después que se halla
en la ocasión, porque aquésta
no hay camino de estorbarla.
Sirva de ejemplo este raro
espectáculo, esta extraña
admiración, este horror,
este prodigio; pues nada
es más, que llegar a ver
con prevenciones tan varias,
rendido a mis pies a un padre,
y atropellado a un monarca.
Sentencia del cielo fue;
por más que quiso estorbarla
él, no pudo; ¿y podré yo,
que soy menor en las canas,
en el valor y en la ciencia,
vencerla?—Señor, levanta,
dame tu mano; que ya
que el cielo te desengaña
de que has errado en el modo
de vencerle, humilde aguarda
mi cuello a que tú te vengues:
rendido estoy a tus plantas.

BAS.:   Hijo, que tan noble acción
            otra vez en mis entrañas

a storm on the ocean;
and (hear me out!) even if my rage
had been a sleeping beast,
my fury a temperate sword,
and my harshness a tranquil calm at sea,
fortune is not overcome
by injustice and revenge,
which, on the contrary, only egg it on all the more;
and so, the man who expects to overcome
his fortune must do so
with prudence and temperateness.
It isn't before the harm arrives
that the man who foresees it protects himself
and guards against it; because, even though
he can, by humble resignation (it's evident),
protect himself from it, this can happen
only after he finds himself
in the actual situation, because there's no way
of preventing it from arriving.
Let this unusual spectacle
be an example, this odd
wonder, this awful situation,
this miracle; because there can't be
a better example than to finally see,
despite all those different precautions,
a father submissive at my feet,
and a monarch trampled upon.
It was the verdict of heaven;
no matter how he tried to prevent it,
he couldn't; and will I,
younger in years
and inferior in merit and learning,
be able to overcome it?—Rise, Sire,
give me your hand; for, now
that heaven undeceives you,
showing you that you erred in your method
of overcoming it, my neck
humbly awaits your revenge:
I fall in submission at your feet.

BAS.: My son—for, such a noble action
       engenders you once again

te engendra, príncipe eres.
A ti el laurel y la palma
se te deben; tú venciste;
corónente tus hazañas.

TODOS: ¡Viva Segismundo, viva!

SEG.:   Pues que ya vencer aguarda
          mi valor grandes vitorias,
          hoy ha de ser la más alta
          vencerme a mí: Astolfo dé
          la mano luego a Rosaura,
          pues sabe que de su honor
          es deuda, y yo he de cobrarla.

AST.:   Aunque es verdad que la debo
          obligaciones, repara
          que ella no sabe quién es;
          y es bajeza y es infamia
          casarme yo con mujer . . .

CLO.:   No prosigas, tente, aguarda;
          porque Rosaura es tan noble
          como tú, Astolfo, y mi espada
          lo defenderá en el campo;
          que es mi hija, y esto basta.

AST.:   ¿Qué dices?

CLO.:   Que yo hasta verla
          casada, noble y honrada,
          no la quise descubrir.
          La historia de esto es muy larga;
          pero, en fin, es hija mía.

AST.:   Pues siendo así, mi palabra
          cumpliré.

SEG.:   Pues porque Estrella
          no quede desconsolada,
          viendo que príncipe pierde
          de tanto valor y fama,
          de mi propia mano yo
          con esposo he de casarla
          que en méritos y fortuna,
          si no le excede, le iguala.
          Dame la mano.

EST.:   Yo gano
          en merecer dicha tanta.

in my loins—you are prince!
To you the laurel and palm
are due; you have conquered;
may your exploits crown you!

ALL.: Long live Segismundo! Long may he live!

SEG.: Since my valor now expects
to win great victories,
today the loftiest of all shall be
a victory over myself: let Astolfo give
his hand at once to Rosaura,
because he knows it is a debt
of honor, and I shall collect it.

AST.: Though it's true that I have
obligations toward her, please note
that she doesn't know who her father was;
and it's vileness and infamy
for me to marry a woman . . .

CLO.: Don't go on, stop, wait;
because Rosaura is as noble
as you, Astolfo, and my sword
will champion her in the field;
for she is my daughter, and that's sufficient.

AST.: What's that you say?

CLO.:   That, before seeing her
married, noble, and respected,
I didn't want to reveal her identity.
The story behind it is a very long one;
but, in a word, she's my daughter.

AST.: Well, that being the case, I'll keep
my word.

SEG.:   Then, so that Estrella
won't remain disconsolate,
seeing herself losing a prince
of such great merit and fame,
with my own hand I
shall wed her to a husband
who, in worth and fortune,
though he doesn't outdo him, is at least his equal.
Give me your hand!

EST.:   I gain
by deserving such great happiness.

SEG.:   A Clotaldo, que leal
          sirvió a mi padre, le aguardan
          mis brazos, con las mercedes
          que él pidiere que le haga.
SOL. 1.°: Si así a quien no te ha servido
          honras, a mí que fui causa
          del alboroto del reino,
          y de la torre en que estabas
          te saqué, ¿qué me darás?
SEG.:   La torre; y porque no salgas
          de ella nunca hasta morir,
          has de estar allí con guardas,
          que el traidor no es menester
          siendo la traición pasada.
BAS.:   Tu ingenio a todos admira.
AST.:   ¡Qué condición tan mudada!
ROS.:   ¡Qué discreto y qué prudente!
SEG.:   ¿Qué os admira? ¿qué os espanta
          si fue mi maestro un sueño,
          y estoy temiendo en mis ansias
          que he de despertar y hallarme
          otra vez en mi cerrada
          prisión? Y cuando no sea,
          el soñarlo sólo basta:
          pues así llegué a saber
          que toda la dicha humana
          en fin pasa como sueño,
          y quiero hoy aprovecharla
          el tiempo que me durare,
          pidiendo de nuestras faltas
          perdón, pues de pechos nobles
          es tan propio el perdonarlas.

SEG.:   My embrace awaits Clotaldo,
        who served my father
        loyally, and so do any favors
        he asks me to do for him.

SOL. 1: If that's the way you honor a man
        who wasn't on your side, what will you give
        me, since I instigated
        the uprising in the kingdom and released you
        from the tower in which you languished?

SEG.:   The tower! And, so that you never
        leave it until you die,
        you shall be kept under guard there,
        because a traitor is no longer needed
        once the treason is over.

BAS.:   We are all amazed at your intelligence!

AST.:   What a change in his nature!

ROS.:   How clever and wise he is!

SEG.:   Why are you surprised? Why are you astonished,
        when my teacher was a dream,
        and in my anxiety I'm afraid
        I may wake up again and find myself
        once more in my locked
        cell? And even if that doesn't happen,
        merely dreaming it might is enough:
        for in that way I came to know
        that all of human happiness
        passes by in the end like a dream,
        and I wish today to enjoy mine
        for as long as it lasts,
        asking pardon for
        our faults, since it so befits
        noble hearts to pardon them!